LECTURES ON DEIXIS

CSLI
Lecture Notes
Number 65

LECTURES ON
DEIXIS

CHARLES J. FILLMORE

CSLI Publications

Center for the Study of
Language and Information
Stanford, California

This book was set by CSLI Publications in Minion, a typeface designed by Robert Slimbach. The book was printed and bound in the United States of America.

Library of Congress Cataloging-in-Publications Data

Fillmore, Charles J.
Lectures on Deixis / Charles J. Fillmore.
p.   cm. – (CSLI lecture notes ; no. 65)
ISBN: 1-57586-006-6 (pbk. : alk. paper).
ISBN: 1-57586-007-4 (hardcover : alk. paper)
1. Grammar, Comparative and general – Deixis.   I. Title.
II. Series.
P299.D44F49   1997
415–dc20   96-35248
CIP

∞ The acid-free paper used in this book meets the minimum requirements of the American National Standard for Information Sciences – Permanence of Paper for Printed Library Materials, ANSI Z39.48-1984.

CSLI was founded early in 1983 by researchers from Stanford University, SRI International, and Xerox PARC to further research and development of integrated theories of language, information, and computation. CSLI headquarters and CSLI Publications are located on the campus of Stanford University.

CSLI Publications reports new developments in the study of language, information, and computation. In addition to lecture notes, our publications include monographs, working papers, revised dissertations, and conference proceedings. Our aim is to make new results, ideas, and approaches available as quickly as possible. Please visit our website at
http://csli-www.stanford.edu/publications/
for comments on this and other titles, as well as for changes and corrections by the author and publisher.

CONTENTS

INTRODUCTION TO THE REPRINTING OF THE DEIXIS LECTURES

The lectures reprinted here were given in Santa Cruz in the summer of 1971, a quarter of a century ago, and have been made available through the Indiana University Club (IUC) from time to time since then. In the preface to the IUC version I stated that I would probably never succeed in reshaping and expanding these lectures into a book because I wouldn't know where to start and I would certainly not know when to stop. That statement continues to hold. I knew I couldn't write something on deixis from scratch, preserving the scope and mood of the Santa Cruz lectures while responding to recent literature on the topics taken up in these lectures, but I thought I could at least remove the most annoying lecture-hall features of the text. But that would have required a major reshaping of the whole thing, and the request that came to me was to publish the lectures more or less as they stood. This means, for example, that instead of giving numbered examples, and referring to numbers whenever I wanted to say something about the same example in different paragraphs, I simply always repeated it. I made a few half-hearted attempts to re-do the lectures in at least this respect, but in the end I gave up.

It would have been to my advantage to make lots of changes. I have, of course, removed a number of embarrassing infelicities, and jokes that I no longer remember the point of, and I have added qualifications here and there. But it would have been a good idea to make a thorough revision of those sections on which I have been criticized, especially the last chapter. Then, since this edition will be the only one many people are likely to see, readers who compare the criticism with the "original" would feel that my critics were foolish and that I was right after all. Laziness, rather than virtue, has kept me from doing that.

There are all sorts of remarks in here about languages that I know nothing about. Most of them were based on my memory of conversations that I had with Summer Institute of Linguistics (SIL) linguists during a visit to SIL centers in Mexico. Nothing I say about languages other than English, and not everything I say about English, should be taken as authoritative.

These lectures were written when Generative Semantics was approaching its peak of popularity—in fact, the Santa Cruz summer sessions were largely devoted to celebrating G.S.—and some of the remarks here and there in these lectures can only be made intelligible by referring to that background. I have, however, removed a number of allusions to views of grammar that would today require explanations that would only detract from the points that were being made.

I even tried to update pronominal reference, and to repopulate the world of my examples in ways that reflected a more current gender awareness, but I have never been able to deal easily with the grammatical consequences of such monstrosities as "(s)he" or "his/her". But I confess to being more than a little surprised at my own practice, just twenty-five years ago.

The main linguistic writings on deixis that I was aware of at the time these lectures were given were Henri Frei (1944), "Systèmes de déictiques," *Acta linguistica* 4:111–129; Roman Jakobson (1957), "Shifters, Verbal Categories, and the Russian Verb," mimeo, but in French translation as chapter 9 of *Essais de linguistique générale* (1963), Paris: Les Editions de Minuit; Uriel Weinreich (1963), "On the Semantic Structures of Language," in Joseph H. Greenberg, ed., *Universals of language*, MIT Press, esp. pp. 123–127; Charles J. Fillmore (1966) "Deictic Categories in the Semantics of 'come'," *Word* 19:208–231; and John Lyons (1968), *Introduction to Theoretical Linguistics*, Cambridge University Press, pp. 275–281. In the psychological literature there was Karl Bühler (1934), *Sprachtheorie*, Jena, esp. pp. 79–148; and Ragnar Rommetveit (1968), *Words, Meanings and Messages: Theory and Experiments in Psycholinguistics*, Academic Press, passim, but esp. pp. 51–54 and 185–197. Discussion of the philosophical issues connected with deixis could be found in Yehoshua Bar-Hillel (1954), "Indexical Expressions," *Mind* 63:359–379; Arthur W. Burks (1948–9), "Icon, Index and Symbol," *Phi-*

losophy and phenomenological research 9:673–689; and Richard M. Gale (1967), "Indexical Signs, Egocentric Particulars, and Token-Reflexive Words," *The Encyclopedia of Philosophy*, Macmillan, 4:151–155. This last included a discussion, with references, of the positions of Bertrand Russell, C.S. Peirce, and Hans Reichenbach. The Burks article is an exegesis of Peirce.

My thinking on deixis occupied a big part of my time when I was a Fellow at the Center for Advanced Study in the Behavioral Sciences in Stanford, 1970–1971. During this period, at the Center and elsewhere, I had valuable conversations on the topics of deixis with Charles Ferguson, David Peizer, Yehoshua Bar-Hillel, Herb and Eve Clark, Bill Geoghegan, and SIL linguists, Barbara Hollenbach, Bill Merrifield, and Carl Rensch; and with a passenger who rode with me between Palo Alto and Santa Cruz as I commuted for the lecture series, Lily Wong, now Lily Wong Fillmore.

The present version owes much to editorial assistance from Susanne Gahl and Collin Baker. I am especially indebted to CSLI Publications' Dikran Karagueuzian for his unending patience; we were both a lot younger when I first agreed to submit these pages to CSLI Publications.

MAY WE COME IN?[1]

What I intend to do in this first lecture is to offer my view of the full linguistic treatment of the meanings of sentences. I take the subject matter of linguistics, in its grammatical, semantic, and pragmatic sub-divisions, to include the full catalogue of knowledge which the speakers of a language can be said to possess about the structure of the sentences in their language, as well as their knowledge of the appropriate use of these sentences, and I take the special task of linguistics to be that of discovering and displaying the principles which underlie such knowledge.

I have chosen to begin this inquiry by examining, as thoroughly as I can, one simple English sentence. This will be my contribution to a hoary and respectable tradition in linguistics, the dissection of very short sentences. Edward Sapir, you will recall, made famous the sentence "The farmer kills the duckling."[2] In his analysis of that sentence he pointed out a number of word-derivational processes in English, and in comparing that sentence with its translations in several other languages, he was able to put on display the wide number of ways in which concepts and relations get lexicalized and grammaticized in the world's languages.

A sentence which gained some currency in linguistic discussions in the mid-sixties was used by Jerrold Katz and Jerry Fodor in their well-known article on the nature of semantic theory.[3] The sentence was,

1. A version of this paper, with the title "May we come in?", appeared in 1973 in the journal *Semiotica* 9:98–115.

2. Edward Sapir, *Language: An Introduction to the Study of Speech* (New York: Harcourt, Brace, and Company, 1921). Knud Lambrecht has reminded me that the unnaturalness of Sapir's sentence is evidenced by the fact that I am among the large number of linguists who quotes the sentence with "killed" rather than "kills", as I, myself, did in the earlier versions of this lecture, including the version published in *Semiotica*. I had somehow unconsciously wished to work with a sentence that lent itself to some level of natural contextualization.

3. Jerrold J. Katz and Jerry A. Fodor, The Structure of a Semantic Theory, *Language* 39: 170–210 (1963).

"The bill is large," and the reader was asked to determine what one could say about the possible meanings of that sentence independently of any imagined context of use. One of their purposes was to indicate what could be meant by the term *ambiguity* from the linguist's point of view. While it is probably true that no actual utterance of the sentence "The bill is large" would be ambiguous in context, independently of context the sentence can be taken as ambiguous in ways associated with the dictionary entry of the word "bill". Their point was that the context "is large" is compatible with either the "payment-due" or the "bird's beak" sense of the noun "bill", and that a purely linguistic description of that sentence would have to show it to be ambiguous in just those two ways. Katz and Fodor claimed that only a complete theory of language use would be capable of disambiguating utterances in context, and since such a theory would have to incorporate all possible knowledge about the universe, its creation is in principle impossible. In order to be clear about what linguists as linguists can say about the meaning of a sentence, we need to act as if we found it written on a piece of paper with no indication of its author, its addressee, or the occasion of its being produced.

Yehoshua Bar-Hillel, in a well-known demonstration of the non-feasibility of machine translation, built much of his argument on the claim that an algorithm for translating from English into some other language would not be able, in a principled way, to make the right choice for the sentence "The box is in the pen."[4] This, he claimed, is because of the polysemy of the word "pen". Any general procedure capable of achieving a contextual resolution of the word's ambiguity in this sentence would have to have access to encyclopedic information, so that while the writing-implement sense of "pen" would be allowed for a sentence like "The ink is in the pen," that interpretation of the word would be disallowed in our sentence about the box. The information

---

4. Yehoshua Bar-Hillel, The Present Status of Automatic Translation of Languages, in *Advances in Computers*, ed. F. L. Alt (New York: Academic Press, 1960), Appendix III, pp. 158–163.

to which the program would need to have access must specify both that in the desired sense of "pen", pens are larger than boxes and can therefore contain them, whereas in the writing-implement sense, pens cannot contain boxes. One cannot expect the designer of a mechanical translation system to be able to foresee the need to classify nouns according to whether they designate things which can be inserted into fountain pens, or into pigpens but not fountain pens, or which are too big to fit into either.

A particularly famous short sentence in the early history of the theory of grammatical transformations is Chomsky's "Sincerity may frighten the boy."[5] This sentence was used to demonstrate the types of grammatical information that the modern linguist needs to be able to deal with. There is, for example, (1) the categorial information that "sincerity" and "boy" are nouns, "may" is a modal auxiliary, "frighten" is a verb, and "the" is an article, (2) the relational information that the subject/predicate relation holds between the word "sincerity" and the phrase "may frighten the boy" and that the verb/direct object relation holds between the word "frighten" and the noun phrase "the boy," (3) the inherent lexical information that, for example, "sincerity" is a singular abstract noun, while the noun "boy" is animate, masculine, and countable, etc., (4) the strict subcategorizational information that the verb "frighten" requires a direct object and that the noun "boy" requires, in the singular, a preceding determiner,[6] and (5) the selectional information that the verb "frighten" requires an animate direct object but is much less restricted with regard to the class of entities which it welcomes as its subject. One could add to this list of information the additional facts that "Sincerity may frighten the boy" says something about the possibility of somebody experiencing an emotion, with the entity named by the direct object of the sentence as the potential expe-

---

5. Noam Chomsky, *Aspects of the Theory of Syntax* (Cambridge, MA: MIT Press, 1965), pp. 63ff.
6. Today a noun's need for a determiner is no longer thought of in terms of strict subcategorization.

riencer of that emotion; and that the verb must be understood statively when its subject is not animate, but can be understood actively if its subject designates something animate, thus making it possible to predict that while the sentence "Sincerity may frighten the boy" is unambiguous, a sentence like "John may frighten the boy" is ambiguous.

It is striking that in all of these demonstrations, the scope of description and explanation has been limited to what can be said about sentences in the abstract. In no case is the sentence viewed as having what the Norwegian psycholinguist Ragnar Rommetveit calls *deictic anchorage*.[7] In no case was any attention paid to how the sentence can be used, to the conditions under which a speaker of English might choose to use it, the role the sentence might play in an ongoing conversation, or the like. It is true that these happen to be sentences whose contextualizations would not be particularly interesting, and in some cases might actually be quite difficult to imagine, but something, at least, might have been noticed about the conditions for using the definite determiner in all of these sentences.

Rather than go into such matters for my predecessors' sentences, I would like to build my discussion of the explanatory domain of linguistics around a sentence which cannot be understood at all apart from considerations of its being anchored in some social context. The sentence I have chosen for this demonstration is simple and short and extremely easy to understand. It is the four-syllable question "May we come in?" I would like to approach our examination of this sentence by way of asking what we might be able to figure out about some real-world situation if the only thing we knew about it was that somebody used the sentence "May we come in?" I said "used the sentence" rather than "pronounced the sentence" to encourage us to consider the speaker's in-good-faith recognition of the conventions of the English language.

Our task is to make explicit everything that we know about the sentence as a linguistic object, and everything that we can know, as speak-

---

7. Ragnar Rommetveit, *Words, Meanings and Messages* (New York: Academic Press, 1968).

ers of English, about the situation, or class of possible situations, in which it might have been uttered. We will be interested, in short, in the grammatical form of the sentence and the meanings and grammatical properties of its words, and in the assumptions we find ourselves making about the speaker of the sentence and about the setting in which it was uttered. I am following my predecessors in considering the sentence in the abstract, rather than by fitting it to an actual context of utterance, but my goals are to see the ways in which the form and meaning of the sentence constrain its possible uses.

There are various possible phonetic realizations of this particular string of words when used to form a sentence of English. I will speak briefly about other variants later, but will begin by considering that rendering of it which has heaviest stress and rising intonation on the last word.

In asking ourselves to consider the sentence as "used" rather than merely "pronounced", we can allow ourselves first of all to disregard the infinite range of possible conditions for the utterance of this sentence which have little to do with the sentence's form and meaning. Somebody who had been asked, for example, to pronounce four English monosyllables putting heavy stress and rising intonation on the last one might have accidentally come up with the four words of our sentence; or a speaker of a foreign language might have been imitating an English utterance he once overheard, understanding nothing of its meaning; or a librarian might have been reading aloud the title of a short story. Since the range of possibilities for "uttering" without "using" this sentence is only trivially constrained by the form of the actual sentence, a serious examination of such possibilities can safely be set aside as irrelevant.

There are, I believe, two major possible ways of using our sentence. In one, the sentence can be used as a request, on the part of its speaker, that its addressee perform a permission-granting act. On the second (and much less likely) interpretation, the sentence is a request for information, an enquiry as to whether the speaker and a companion already have permission to do something. I will begin by considering the first interpretation.

If we assume that the sentence was uttered in conformity with the system of linguistic conventions whose character we are trying to make explicit, we will probably find ourselves imagining a situation involving some kind of enclosure, call it E, and at least three beings, call them A, B, and C. One of these, A, is a speaker of English and is the utterer of our sentence; one of them, B, is believed by A to be a speaker of English and is the addressee of our sentence; the third, C, is a companion of A. In using the word "beings" rather than the word "persons", I have C in mind, since C might not be a person but might be, for example, A's pet beaver.

We further assume, in picturing the situation in which our sentence could have served as a permission-requesting utterance, that A believes that A and C are outside the enclosure E; that A believes B, the addressee, to be inside E; that A has an interest in gaining admission to E, in C's company; and that A believes that B has the authority–or represents somebody who has the authority–to decide whether or not A and C may enter E. We further understand that the uttering of this sentence is an act which socially requires B to do something–in particular, to say something–it being understood that what B says as a response to the question will count as authorizing or forbidding the move into E on the part of A and his[8] companion C. We know, too, what would count as an authorizing or forbidding act on the part of B. For example, we would know what to make of it if B, on hearing our sentence, were to say, "Sure."

These, then, are the main things that we might find ourselves imagining on learning about a particular situation that somebody uttered the sentence "May we come in?" Actually, if we could assume that people usually know where they are and who they are speaking to, we could give a more basic interpretation by eliminating the fuss about A's beliefs. The scene is one in which A and C are outside some enclosure E,

---

8. These lectures were written at a time when the pronoun "he" was used as a general third-person pronoun. Or maybe it would be more accurate to say that they were written at a time when we usually peopled our illustrations with males.

B is inside E and has gatekeeping authority, and A is asking B for permission for A and C to enter E.

Actual situations in which utterances of this sentence get used may depart from this description in several ways and for several reasons. There were references in my description to things which A believes; some of A's beliefs may be mistaken. There were references, in my description to how A feels; A, of course, may be speaking insincerely. And, of course, the number of A's addressees may be greater than one and the number of A's companions may be greater than one. And, with a little imagination, it would be possible to set up other spatial arrangements of the participants in this scene.

As linguists we need to ask what it is about the structure of the sentence "May we come in?" that makes it possible for any speaker of English to come up with essentially the same sort of description as the one I just suggested. A successful linguistic description of English ought to make it possible to "compute" the details of such a description from a grammatical and lexical description of the sentence. What we have to work with are the four words and an extremely limited amount of structure: the sentence is a question, its subject is the pronoun "we", its main verb is "come", it contains, in association with this verb the modal auxiliary "may", and the verb "come" comes with a directional complement "in".

Let us take the words one at a time, beginning with "may". The word "may", when used as a modal auxiliary, has three functions that will interest us here, and these I will refer to as its (1) epistemic, (2) pragmatic, and (3) magical functions. In its epistemic function, it is used in possibility-asserting expressions such as "He may not understand you." In its pragmatic function, it is used in sentences uttered as parts of permission-granting or permission-seeking acts, such as "You may come in now." In its magical function it is used in the expression of wishes, blessings, and curses, such as "May all your troubles be little ones" or "May you spend eternity roller-skating on cobblestones."

In its magical use, this modal only occurs in initial position, and "may" is in the initial position in our sentence. The curse I invented, recast with "may" in post-subject position, becomes "You may spend eternity roller-skating on cobblestones." Such a sentence would count as a warning or a gloomy prediction, but not as a bona fide curse. I have said that our sentence is to be construed as a question, and it is clear, I think, that the function of asking a question is incompatible with the function of issuing a magical wish. I assume, in fact, that the sequence of words I have taken as my example cannot be given a "magical" interpretation. (The curse interpretation is clearly not a question, in spite of its form. One cannot imagine a conversation of the sort: A: "May you spend eternity roller-skating on cobblestones." B: "Yes.")

Certain sentences with "may" are ambiguous between the epistemic and the pragmatic functions of that modal. One example is "John may leave the room." The person who utters that sentence may either, in doing so, be authorizing somebody named John to leave the room, or he may be expressing his belief in the possibility of that person's leaving the room at some time in the future. It is clear, however, that the epistemic and pragmatic senses are not both potentially present in every non-magical use of "may". It happens that these two uses of the modal are associated with two grammatically quite distinct sets of contextual possibilities, and instances of ambiguity with respect to these two senses are instances of accidental overlap of these two context sets. In support of this claim, I will content myself with merely giving examples. It is probably immediately clear that the permission-granting sense is completely absent if what follows is in the perfect aspect. The sentence "John may have left the room," for example, does not permit a pragmatic interpretation such as, "I hereby give John permission to have left the room." It is probably also clear that the possibility-expressing sense is absent from "May John leave the room?"; that question does not permit an epistemic interpretation such as, "Is it possible that John will leave the room?"

The fact that the pragmatic sense of "may" does not show up in the perfect aspect, whereas the possibility sense does, has to do with the fact that the semantic complements of the former are to be understood as acts, while those of the latter are to be understood as eventualities in general. The fact that the epistemic sense does not show up in questions, however, appears to be lexically idiosyncratic. The modal "might" can indeed have an epistemic sense in questions, as in "Might John leave the room?" That question can be interpreted as meaning "Is it possible that John will leave the room?"

The reason we know that our sentence "May we come in?" concerns the permission-granting use of "may" is that our sentence is a question, and neither the magical nor the epistemic sense of the modal is compatible with the sentence that is a question. We are left with the assumption that it is used in its pragmatic sense, and therefore that it is used in a social situation involving permission-granting in some way.

Permission-granting situations involve two parties, the person or persons accepted as having authority to grant the permission, and the person or persons whose actions are to be authorized. A sentence with pragmatic "may" may be uttered performatively,[9] in which case the utterance is a part of a permission-seeking or permission-granting act, or it may be uttered nonperformatively. In the latter case, it is a statement or question about somebody's having permission to do something. It is the performative use of our sentence which I had in mind when I lined up the details of the situation involving beings A, B, and C and the enclosure E. In the performative use, our question permits the paraphrase "Do you give us permission to come in?"; and a non-performative interpretation permits the paraphrase, "Do we have permission to come in?" I will postpone until a little later my discussion of a possible non-performative interpretation of this sentence.

In a performative utterance of a pragmatic "may" sentence, the possessor of authority is taken to be the speaker if the sentence is an assertion, but the addressee if the sentence is a question. Thus, the speaker of "John may leave the room" is, in producing the sentence performatively, authorizing John to leave the room. The sentence we are exam-

---

9. May I be forgiven for describing the question as also an instance of a "performative use"? It is a part of a conversational exchange for which a performance, rather than information, is being sought.

ining, however, is a question, and in uttering a question with pragmatic "may", the speaker is acknowledging the addressee's authority with respect to the permission-granting gesture. This alternation of the authority role between the speaker of an assertion and the addressee of a question must be accounted for in terms of general principles of conversation and general principles in the logic of questions and answers. Without going into the details, there are many instances in two-party discourse of role switching between speaker and addressee. The most obvious switch is that between the two conversation-participant pronouns, as in these exchanges:

"I did a good job." – "No, you didn't."

"Have you seen him?" – "Yes, I have."

The interchanged roles may be implicit, not linked to any specific material in the surface sentence. For example, in "Did John seem angry?" the question means, "Did you perceive John as angry?"; in the assertion "John seemed angry," the meaning is that I (or a group including me) perceived John as angry. There are examples of speaker/addressee reversals in the semantic interpretation of an unchanging lexical item, as seen, for example, in the use of the demonstrative "this" in opening utterances on the telephone. If a telephone conversation begins with the utterance "This is Chuck Fillmore," you interpret it as meaning "I am Chuck Fillmore." If it begins with "Is this Chuck Fillmore?" you take it as meaning "Are you Chuck Fillmore?"[10] In short, if A asks B a question, A acknowledges B's authority to answer the question, and B, in trying to answer the question, acknowledges that acknowledgment. Any of the ways in which A's sentence assigns separate roles to speaker and addressee must have those assignments reversed in B's contribution to the same conversation.

In a performative utterance of a sentence like "John may leave the room," the speaker of the sentence is the authority with respect to the

---

10. This usage is apparently limited to American English.

permission-granting act which a performance of that sentence constitutes. If that sentence is, as it is, an authorized answer to the question
"May John leave the room?" it follows that the addressee of the question has the same role as the speaker of the corresponding assertion.
Given these facts about role-switching, you can see that a problem
could arise when the subject of a sentence with pragmatic "may" is the
pronoun "we", a word which is capable of referring to a group that includes both the speaker and the addressee.

So far we have seen how a speaker of English is able to reach certain
conclusions about our sentence: from the fact that it is a question and
contains the modal "may", (1) it involves the permission-granting sense
of "may" and (2) it is the addressee of the sentence who is taken as having the right to grant the desired permission.

In the sentence "May we come in?" the pronoun "we" has to be interpreted as exclusive (somebody else and me, not you and me), and
that was in fact the reason we were forced to imagine three beings in a
situation compatible with this particular utterance. The individual we
have been calling c is the other being included in the set of beings referred to as "we" and distinct from the addressee b. In our sentence,
this fact about "we" is overdetermined, since the verb associated with
our modal is the verb "come"; but if we replace "come" by "go", we will
see, I think, that there is a relationship between the exclusive character
of the pronoun and the performative interpretation of the question.
When the question "May we go in?" is used as a permission-seeking utterance, it is more natural to think of the pronoun as referring to a
group which does not include the addressee, for the reason that in the
permission-granting situation, the person with authority and the person or persons seeking permission are typically distinct. On the other
hand, when the question "May we go in?" is interpreted as meaning
"Do we have permission to go in?" there is no difficulty in construing
the pronoun either exclusively or inclusively.

So far, then, this is what we know: from the fact that our sentence is a
question having "may" as its modal, we know that it has to do with a
permission-requesting situation. From the fact that it is a question

rather than an assertion, we know that it is the addressee, and not the speaker, who has the authority role. And from a general understanding of permission-granting situations, wc know that the person having authority is distinct from the persons who need and seek permission to enter, and that therefore the pronoun "we" must be being used in the sense which is exclusive of the addressee. (To many people this argument is not convincing, because they claim that they can imagine a situation in which one person asks another "May we go in?" and means "Do you now give you and me permission to enter?" Such people would not disagree on the ultimate interpretation of the question at hand, but would disagree on the contribution of "may" to the conclusion about the exclusivity of "we".)

We turn now to the third word, the main verb of the sentence, the word "come". We notice first of all that it is an action verb, and therefore the activity it identifies qualifies as something for which it makes sense to speak of granting permission. If our sentence were something like "May we understand your proposal?" we would have had to reject it as an ill-formed pragmatic-"may" question, since one does not speak of needing permission to understand something. For that sentence to be acceptable at all, it would have to be construed as something like "May we be given more information about your proposal so that we can understand it?"

As an action verb, furthermore, "come" is not an "achievement" verb. If our sentence were "May we succeed on this project?" it would have to be rejected as an ill-formed pragmatic-"may" question, since "succeed", as an achievement verb, refers to attaining a particular outcome of an unidentified activity, something for which a request for permission is incoherent.

The verb "come", secondly, is lexically simple with respect to the type of activity it designates. In this way it differs from a verb like "swim", which has associated with it both the idea of motion and an understanding of a particular manner of motion.

If our sentence had been "May we swim in?" we would have had to point out that it could be used in two distinct permission-seeking situations. Suppose, for illustration, that the speaker and his companion were swimming in a stream that entered a cave, and they were addressing a person guarding the entrance to the cave. In that case there could be no question of their needing permission to swim–they are already swimming–and they are merely asking for permission to move into the cave while continuing to swim. The sentence, in that case, would have heavy stress on "in". Suppose, on the other hand, that the speaker and his companion have already been granted permission to enter the cave, and they wish to know whether they may do this by way of the stream, that is, by swimming into it. In that case, it is already understood that they have permission to move into the cave, and what they are seeking is permission to do so by swimming. And in that case the sentence would have heavy stress on "swim".

The verb "come", I suggested, does not have this sort of lexical complexity, and so there is not any ambiguity about aspects of the situation for which permission is needed. The question we are examining, you will recall, has heavy stress and rising intonation on the final word "in". In the sentence with the double-barreled verb "swim" the de-stressing of the main verb is associated with a presupposition, namely, the presupposition that "we" are already swimming. The de-stressing of the lexically simple "come", on the other hand, has no analogous presupposition associated with it.

The verb "come" has other sorts of complexities, however, and this is where we arrive at the topic of deixis. As it happens, the description of the presuppositional structure of motion sentences containing this verb requires reference to all three of the major grammaticalized types of deixis–person, place, and time.

First, a digression on time. In speaking of temporal indications in the semantics of natural languages, it is necessary to distinguish the coding time, roughly, the time of the speech act, from the reference time, the point or period of time that is being referred to or focused on in the sentence. (There is more, but that can wait.) We can see how both of these types of temporal concepts can figure in the description of a single sentence by considering the sentence "John was here last

Tuesday." The reference time is reflected in the choice of tense on the verb and is indicated by the phrase "last Tuesday". The coding time is involved in the interpretation of "last Tuesday" as, say, the Tuesday of the calendar week which precedes the calendar week which includes the moment of speech, and in the interpretation of "here" as meaning "the place where the speaker finds himself at the time of pronouncing the sentence".

The role of deictic categories in the interpretation of sentences with our verb "come" may be observed with sentences of the form:

x came to y at t

where x is the moving entity, y is the destination, and t is the reference time. For this example I have put t in the past for ease of exposition. It happens that sentences of the form "x came to y at t" are appropriate just in case any of the following conditions obtains:

1. The speaker is at y at coding time.
2. The addressee is at y at coding time.
3. The speaker is at y at reference time.
4. The addressee is at y at reference time.

To see that this is so, take "John", "the office", and "yesterday morning" as values of x, y, and t respectively. A sentence like "John came to the office yesterday morning" is appropriate under any of the four conditions just indicated. That is, it is a sentence that I can say appropriately if I am in the office when I say it, if you are in the office when I say it to you, if I was in the office yesterday morning when John came, or if you were in the office yesterday morning when John came.

Sentences with the verb "come" are, then, potentially ambiguous in at least four ways,[11] in an unusual sense of ambiguity related to what

---

11. This description does not cover all uses of the motion-verb "come". It has special uses when the motion referred to is motion on the part of both speaker and hearer, a use in which the destination is thought of as somebody's "home base", and in a special and very interesting use to which it can be put in third-person narrative. The full story is told in the chapter "Coming and Going" in this volume.

users of the sentence can be said to presuppose. It is not true that every such sentence with "come" is ambiguous in these four ways, however, because limitations on these appropriateness conditions appear when we substitute for the x and y of the formula expressions of person deixis and place deixis, respectively. For example, if I say, "I came there yesterday morning," it cannot be that I am there now, because "there" is by definition a place where I am not now located, and it cannot be that I was already there yesterday morning when I came. Only interpretations 2 and 4 are possible.

But now what are we to say about our sentence? We have seen, from the fact that we are dealing with permission-granting "may" in an interrogative sentence, that our pronoun "we" is exclusive of the addressee. That same conclusion could also have been reached by noticing its occurrence with the verb "come". "Come" is a verb of locomotion which indicates a change of location from some point of origin to some destination, this latter conceived of as a place where the speaker or addressee is located at the time of the speech act or at the reference time. In a permission-seeking utterance with the modal "may", a definite reference time is lacking, and that leaves open only those possibilities that refer to the participants' location at the time of the speech act. Since the pronoun "we" has to include the speaker but does not have to include the addressee, we are forced to conclude that "we" is exclusive: since the addressee must be at the place of destination in order for the use of this sentence to be appropriate, he cannot be included in the group seeking to move toward that destination. Again our analysis supports the picture we had at the beginning: of A on the outside, speaking on behalf of himself and C, also on the outside, and addressing the insider, B.

(There is a possibility for our question that I have not yet mentioned, and that is the possibility that it is uttered in a context in which the preceding discourse has provided a (future) reference time. Understood in that way, the situation with A, B, C, and E that I set up at the beginning would have to be modified. On this new interpretation, it is not required that B be inside E at the time of the speech act, but only that A assumes that B will be inside E at the time of the movement of A and C into E.)

The English verb "come", like its partner "go", is one of the few verbs of motion which require a destination complement in syntactically complete sentences. In our case the destination complement has the form "in", which we may take as an ellipsis for something like "into the place". Since "in" as a destination particle means something paraphrasable as "to a place which is inside", its occurrence in this sentence can be said to ascribe to the destination which the speaker has in mind the information that it is a part of the interior of some sort of enclosure. This is different from whatever interpretation we would have given if our demonstration sentence had been something like "May we come up?" "May we come through?" "May we come over?" or the like. The information that the destination is in some sort of an enclosure, together with the information that the addressee is at the time of the speech act located at the destination of the movement, is what imposes the understanding that the moving entities have as their point of origin a location which is not within that enclosure, and this contributes to our picture of the speaker and his companion being outside of an enclosure, and the addressee being inside it.[12]

The *illocutionary act potential* of a sentence must be studied in the context of the systems of rules or conventions that we might choose to call discourse rules, a subset of which might be called conversation rules. We have seen, in what has already been said about the illocutionary force of our example sentence, that it is not to be construed as a request for information, but as a request for the addressee to "perform" in some way. It is usable as a way of getting the conversation partner to perform the needed permission-granting or permission-denying act. In the sense that a question like "Shall we come in?" can be taken as a request for a command, the question "May we come in?" can be taken as a request for permission. Because of its role in a changing interper-

---

12. A more complete story of the fourth word would recognize that "in" is a preposition that permits the omissibility of its complement if information about it is "given" in the context. See Charles J. Fillmore, Pragmatically Controlled Zero Anaphora, *Papers from the Twelfth Annual Meeting of the Berkeley Linguistics Society*, (1986), pp. 95–107.

sonal situation, a complete description of the sentence must specify the social and physical conditions which must be satisfied in order for it to be used appropriately. For various reasons these may be stated as belief conditions which must be satisfied by the utterer of the sentence in order for us to acknowledge that it has been uttered in good faith.

We have agreed that the speaker must believe that the addressee is inside E, that he and his companion are outside E, and that B is a person capable of authorizing admission into E. We will also agree, I believe, that in the most straightforward interpretation of a permission-seeking sentence, the speaker wants to do what he is asking permission to do, and that he believes he needs to get this permission before he can properly do what he wants to do. By considering these various types of appropriateness conditions for utterances, we are able to recognize various ways in which utterances of the sentence can be said to be deviant. The sentence can be uttered mistakenly, in case the speaker's beliefs are incorrect, or it may be uttered insincerely, in case the belief conditions are not satisfied or in case the speaker does not really desire what his uttering the sentence implies that he desires.

It is in an effort to understand the nature of discourse, I believe, where we can make most explicit the principles which govern the appropriateness of utterance types, because it is there that these principles can be used to make judgments about the appropriateness and the "force" of utterances given their contexts.

Consider our sentence. A may be mistaken in his belief that he is outside the enclosure E, and this will become apparent to him, and to us, if B's response is, "Well, fellows, it looks to me like you're already in." A may be mistaken in his belief about the location of B. He will realize that if he hears, from an unexpected direction, the reply "Yoohoo, here I am; go right on in." A may be mistaken in his belief that B is the proper authority, and this he will learn if he hears B say, "Don't ask me!" And A may be mistaken in his belief that he needs permission to enter, and he will find that out if B's answer is something like, "Of course, why do you ask?"

The sentence can be used "insincerely" in two ways. It may be used politely, in which case the assumptions associated with the sentence about the social dominance (on this occasion) of the addressee are intended as a polite social gesture, or the sentence may be used ironically, as in cases where the suggested dominance relation is clearly contradicted by the realities of the situation. The word "insincere" is not a particularly happy way to characterize the polite use; I refer merely to the fact that the belief conditions about the status of the addressee are not exactly satisfied. An example of the ironic use can be seen in the situation in which prison wardens address the question to a prisoner in his cell, or in the case of a pair of aggressive encyclopedia salesmen who have already entered the living room.

The conversation rules of the language govern not only the conditions under which it is appropriate to perform the permission-requesting utterance of the type we have been examining, but they must also determine the principles by which a speaker of English is able to recognize appropriate responses to the request. If the question is used in absolutely its most straightforward way—a rare occurrence, I would guess—the normal affirmative answer would be something like "Okay" or "Yes, you may."

There is something slightly rude about these answers, and it is interesting to see why this should be so. The questioner is saying something like "I would like to enter the place where you are, and I am asking you to give me permission to do that." One would think that an answer that means, in effect, "I hereby grant you the permission that you requested" should exactly satisfy the request, but the fact is, it does so in an unpleasing way. In the social dialect of English that most of us probably feel most comfortable with, one of the things we attempt to maintain in conversational interaction is the masking of social stratification. The questioner, in asking "May we come in?" is exposing his desire to enter the enclosure containing the addressee, and is imputing a status of authority for this occasion to the addressee. What a straightforward answer like "Yes, you may" does is acknowledge this status difference, and that is what would make it seem rude in a community where conversational politeness is expected. Oddly, a polite answer to a request for permission doesn't have the appearance of a permission-granting utterance at all, but of a command. More polite than the answer "Yes, you may" are answers like "Yes, please do," or "Come in, by all means."

If one wonders why a command is more polite, in this context, than a simple permission-granting utterance, one way of looking at it is this. In making the request, A has exposed to B his desire to enter E; on ordering A to enter, B, by return, is exposing to A B's desire to have A enter E, and this is because of appropriateness conditions associated with commands. The more polite answer, in spite of the fact that stratification masking is not explicitly achieved, is the one which shows that B not only tolerates but desires the admission to E on the part of A and C.[13]

That a command can serve technically as an answer to a request for permission is related not only to the appropriateness conditions for commands having to do with the speaker's desires, but also to the fact that there is a logical entailment relationship between commands and permission-grantings. The theory of well-formed conversations, if it is to show in a principled way what sorts of things qualify as answers to questions, must include or have access to a set of meaning postulates for natural language that would indicate, for example, the entailment relationship between expressions containing the pairs of concepts RE-QUIRE and PERMIT, DESIRE and TOLERATE, or NECESSARY and POSSIBLE.

I have spoken so far about the performative interpretation of our sample sentence. In its non-performative sense, our question comes as a request for information rather than as a request for action. In the non-performative interpretation, the question means "Do you know whether we have permission to come in?" (I believe there are many speakers of English who do not have this interrogative use of permission-"may".) The main difference in the situation which wel-

---

13. There is something incomplete about this explanation. It seems that commands are not invariably the more polite way to answer a request for permission, but only when the activity in question could be construed as an inconvenience to the permission-granter. A polite reply to "May I leave now?" is not "Please do, by all means."

comes the sentence on the interpretation we are now giving it is that A believes B to have information rather than authority and that the sentence is uttered in an information-seeking rather than a permission-seeking situation. The discourse principles associated with possible answers to "May we come in?" when construed non-performatively are, I think, fairly easy to determine, and I won't say anything about them except to point out that the response "Okay" would show that the answerer construed the question as a performative.

So far I have been considering only that phonetic rendering of our question which has heavy stress and rising intonation on the last word, and I promised to say something about other possible renderings of this particular string of words. I already pointed out differences in stress placement potential between our sentence and the question "May we swim in?" I said that for that sentence, when the word "in" is stressed, the presupposition is made that the speaker and his companion are already swimming, and that when the word "swim" is stressed, it is presupposed that they have already been given permission to enter. The verb "come", as I pointed out, does not give us this option, because this word is a pure motion word that does not have associated with it any notion of means, medium, or manner of movement.

I assume that there are two functions of contrastive stress: one of these has to do with the assumption of a contextually relevant proposition that can be constructed out of the destressed portion of the sentence, in which some unspecified but perhaps contextually understood constituent occupies the position represented by the contrastively stressed element; the other occurs in utterances that a speaker is repeating because his addressee did not hear or did not believe what was said the first time, with the heavy stress assigned to the constituent which the speaker is trying to be clear about. For our sentence, the second of these functions allows the placement of heavy stress on any of our four words. In the first function, heavy stress may occur on any of the words except "come", but most naturally, I suppose, on the pronoun.

Let me now summarize the various kinds of facts which must, I suggest, be included in a fully developed system of linguistic description.[14]

1. The linguistic description of a language must characterize for each lexical item in the language
    a. the grammatical constructions in which it can occur,
    b. the grammatical processes to which it is subject in each relevant context,
    c. the grammatical processes which its presence in a construction determines, and
    d. information about speech act conditions, conversation rules, and semantic interpretation which must be associated in an idiosyncratic way with the lexical item in question;
2. it must contain a component for calculating the complete semantic and pragmatic description of a sentence given its grammatical structure and information associated with these lexical items;
3. it must be able to draw on a theory of illocutionary acts, in terms of which the calculations of 2 are empowered to provide a full account of the illocutionary act potential of each sentence;
4. it must be able to draw on a theory of discourse which relates the use of sentences in social and conversational situations; and
5. it must be able to draw on a theory of conversational reasoning by means of which such judgments as the success of an argument or the appropriateness of elements in conversations can be deduced.

---

14. I would say this very differently today, since I now follow a grammatical framework in which everything involves static descriptions of grammatical constructions, and in which sentences are licensed by the unification of the constructions which underlie them. I could not "correct" this section without writing an additional chapter that would motivate the language in the "correction".

In this lecture I have argued that there are principles of linguistic description which should be geared in some way to deictically anchored sentences. Very little of previous linguistic theory has paid attention to this phenomenon. In my succeeding lectures I will emphasize the deictic aspects of language, exploring in turn notions of space, time, movement, the ongoing discourse, and the reflexes in language of the identity of the participants in a conversation and their relationships to each other. My goal in this lecture series is to show how the phenomena of deixis impose a number of serious empirical, conceptual, and notational problems for grammatical theory, and to try to solve some of them.

(Much of this chapter and the next one would be very different if they had been written after such publications as Clark (1973),[1] Herskovits (1985),[2] Jackendoff (1983),[3] Lyons (1977),[4] Miller and Johnson-Laird (1976),[5] Talmy (1985),[6] and Vandeloise (1986/1991).[7] Regrettably, no updating attempt has been made.)

I said in the first lecture that one of my goals in these talks was to become clear about the ways in which the grammars of natural languages reflect what Rommetveit calls the "deictic anchorage" of sentences–an understanding of the roles sentences can serve in social situations occurring in space and time. Frequently, as I tried to show in that lecture, a sentence uttered in context can only be fully interpreted if we know something about the situation in which it has been used; in many cases, then, understanding a sentence out of context involves knowing the class of situations in which it could be appropriately uttered, and knowing what effect it could be expected to have in that situation.

One of the sub-categories of deixis is *place deixis*, having to do with

1. Herbert H. Clark, Space, time, semantics and the child, in *Cognitive Development and the Acquisition of Language,* ed. T. E. Moore (New York: Academic Press, 1973).

2. Annette Herskovits, *Language and Spatial Cognition* (Cambridge: Cambridge University Press, 1985).

3. Ray Jackendoff, *Semantics and Cognition* (Cambridge, MA: MIT Press, 1983) Chapter 9 is "Semantics of spatial expressions".

4. John Lyons, *Semantics,* 2 volumes (Cambridge: Cambridge University Press, 1977) Chapter 15 is "Deixis, space and time".

5. George A. Miller and Philip N. Johnson-Laird, *Language and Perception* (Cambridge: Cambridge University Press, 1976).

6. Leonard Talmy, How language structures space, in *Spatial Orientation: Theory, Research, and Application,* ed. Herbert L. Pick, Jr. and Linda P. Acredolo (New York: Plenum Press, 1985).

7. Claude Vandeloise, *Spatial Prepositions: A Case Study from French* (Chicago: University of Chicago Press, 1991). (Original publication in 1986 as *L'espace en français: Sémantique des prépositions spatiales, Editions du Seuil*)

the linguistic expression of the speaker's perception of his position in three-dimensional space. A second subcategory of deixis is *time deixis*, having to do with the position in time of the speech act. Before I go on to the topics of place and time *deixis*, I plan to devote two lectures to *non-deictic* conceptions of space and time.

The difference between deictic and non-deictic conceptions can be understood by an analogy. Consider the difference between a sculptured representation of a human figure, set up in the middle of a courtyard, and a photograph of a human figure. The sculpture does not represent any particular observer's point-of-view, but the photograph does. The photograph does because the camera had to be positioned at a particular place in front of or to the side of, above or below, or on the same level as, the model.

Sometimes the same linguistic material can have both non-deictic and deictic functions. One example is the word "left". In a sentence like "My sister stood at the general's left side," we have an example of the non-deictic use of the word "left". The location of the speaker at the time of the speech act is completely irrelevant. The situation is quite different for a sentence like "What's that shiny object over there, just to the left of the cypress tree?" In this second case, the location in space of the participants in the conversation is absolutely essential to an interpretation of the question.

I will deal today with spatial notions that have no connection with the observer's point of view, as in the sentence about my sister and the general. Knowing what it means to stand at the general's left side requires knowing something about how a general's body is designed; it requires no special understanding at all about the location or orientation of the person who utters the sentence.

A number of writers who have interested themselves in the semantic structure of the system of locative prepositions in English have noticed that prepositions can be grouped together and distinguished from each other in ways that correspond to the *ascription* of different *dimensionality* properties to the entity named by the following noun or noun phrase. In particular, the preposition "at" is said to ascribe no particular dimensionality to the referent of its associated noun, the preposition "on" is said to ascribe to the referent of its complement the property of being a line or a surface, and the preposition "in" is said to ascribe to the referent of its complement the notion of a bounded two-dimensional or three-dimensional space. Consider phrases like "at the intersection" "on the line" "on the page" "on the wall" "in the city" "in the kitchen".

Frequently a single noun has different interpretations depending on what dimensionality property is associated with the accompanying preposition.[8] Using examples borrowed from Leech (1975),[9] I offer "at the corner" which means near or in contact with the intersection or meeting of two straight lines–or two streets; "on the corner" which locates something as being in contact with a particular part of the surface of some angular two-dimensional figure or three-dimensional object; while "in the corner" is an expression in which the noun "corner" is used to indicate a portion of three-dimensional space–in particular, a part of the interior of, say, a room.

Or consider the difference between the understanding of the noun "island" when it is used with the preposition "on" or the preposition "in". If something is said to be "in the island", the noun is used as indicating merely a bounded geographical area; if something is said to be "on the island", the word "island" is taken as naming something perceived as a three-dimensional object in three-dimensional space. Notice that there is nothing particularly odd about the phrase "on Guam", because it is easy to conceive of Guam as a separable three-dimensional object that things said to be "on Guam" are on the surface of; it is odd, however, to speak of something as being "on Australia" or "on Greenland".

Leech points out that the noun "grass" is used differently in the two

---

8. That's not actually the way I'd like to say it. Rather than claiming that "corner" is general enough to support the three interpretations suggested in this discussion, I would prefer to say that the word is ambiguous, and that the prepositions serve to welcome one or another of the word's senses. The fact that some languages have different lexical items for these distinct senses may be seen as supporting the latter view.

9. Geoffrey Leech, *Towards a Semantic Description of English* (London: Longman, 1975).

expressions "in the grass" and "on the grass". In the former the grass is thought of as being a relevantly three-dimensional space, which would imply that one has in mind either very small objects or fairly tall grass.

A number of nouns in our language seem to have their dimensionality properties built in, because they are more or less limited to occurring with one or another of the two prepositions "on" or "in". For example, "lawn" and "yard". We speak of children playing "on the lawn" or "in the yard", but not as playing "in the lawn", or "on the yard" in the same meanings. The noun "lawn" is generally used only to indicate a surface, but the noun "yard" names a bounded area and not specifically a surface.

Being located on the surface of this planet calls for "on" if we use the word "earth" but "in" if we use the word "world". The word "earth" names a three-dimensional object in three-dimensional space, as many things about the syntax of that word show: what is "in the earth" is in the *interior* of a three-dimensional object, what is "on the earth" is on the *surface* of a three-dimensional object. (Compare: "Where in the world have you been?" and "Where on earth have you been?") We can speak of the distance between the earth and the sun, but not of the distance between the world and the sun.

The concepts that are apparently needed for covering this three-way system are simple location, surface, and interior. John Catford's terms are neutral, exterior, and interior.[10] Location of something in contact with a surface calls for the preposition "on". Simple location, with no reference to surface or interior, calls for "at". The word "surface" is perhaps not too apt, since what I have in mind includes a line, as in "on the line", "on the edge", "on the border", etc. Catford's word exterior doesn't particularly help with that, either.

The surface versus interior distinction seems to be very similar to what distinguishes the adessive/allative/ablative cases in Finnish from the inessive/illative/elative cases—except that in Finnish there seems

---

10. John Catford, Learning a Language in the Field: Problems of Linguistic Relativity, *Modern Language Journal* 53.5 (1969).

not to be a category that corresponds to the simple or "at"-type locative of English. Robert Austerlitz (in lecture) has distinguished the two systems as *unbounded* and *bounded*, the bounded understood as having a boundary that makes it possible for something to be said to be inside it. Some nouns can presumably be used with either of these case categories, but, as with English "lawn" and "yard", there are some which are limited to one or the other. The word for countryside, according to Austerlitz, occurs only with the adessive etc. cases, the word for forest occurring only with the inessive etc. cases.

John Catford (1969) has shown that the Kabardian system subdivides the interior relationship into four sub-categories, distinguishing them in this way: there is one for horizontally bounded spaces, such as courtyards and boxes; one for lower-bounded spaces, such as holes and pockets; one for upper-bounded spaces, such as houses and rooms; and one for filled spaces such as lakes and crowds.

The typical kind of locating expression in a language is one which indicates the location of one object with respect to some other object. The simplest kinds of locating expressions that we have examined so far do nothing more than impute a certain dimensionality to the reference object. Objects, areas, and spaces can be thought of as having extremities and parts, and a language provides separate words for these. A line has ends, a surface can have an edge, the three-dimensional space satisfying certain space conditions has corners, a middle part, and so on.

The locative expressions I have mentioned so far place something essentially inside or in contact with the reference object or reference area. It is also possible to introduce the concept of relative distance, and refer to one object as being near to or far from the reference object. "She was near the general."

Up to this point I have spoken of the reference objects only in terms of their dimensionality, or in terms of whether it is possible to characterize them as having surfaces or interiors. An extremely important set of spatial notions has to do with whether a reference object can be said to have some sort of orientation in space. Since all of the well-known natural languages have developed on this earth, certain notions of spatial orientation common to all human beings, possibly by virtue of their having semi-circular canals in their inner ears, can be counted on as occurring in the semantic organization of lexical items in all languages. These are, first of all, the up/down orientation that is determined by the direction of gravitational forces as perceived on this earth, and two horizontal axes that we can refer to as front/back and left/right. It is important to realize that for a thing to have an up/down orientation, it must be conceived of as permanently or typically or symbolically oriented in a fixed way with respect to the direction of the pull of gravity. A thing can have a vertical or up/down orientation without having either of the two possible horizontal orientations, as, for example, a cylindrical water-tower. A thing can have a front/back orientation, as for example, a missile moving in outer space, without having either an up/down orientation or a left/right orientation. The left/right orientation, however, is possible for an object only if that object has *both* a vertical or up/down orientation *and* a front/back orientation.

Words that are used for locating objects along the vertical axis with respect to a reference object include, in English, the positions "above", "below", "over", "under", and "beneath." Whether two objects are positioned as being at different positions along the same vertical axis does not depend on how either of the objects is oriented.

I mentioned earlier that English has words for extremities and parts of objects, as with words like "end", "edge", and "corner"; there also are names and modifiers for vertically oriented extremities and parts of objects, such as "top" and "bottom", "upper", and "lower". Notice that the same words "top" and "bottom" name both extremities and parts. If something is "on the top of x", it is in contact with x's upper surface; if something is "in the top of x", it is understood as being contained in the uppermost portion or segment of x.

Many of the expressions by which we locate one object with respect to some other object impute to that second or reference object some sort of horizontal orientation. One of the surfaces of many animals and artifacts is regarded as having a special orientational priority. The word in English for what I have in mind is "front". For animate beings having a certain degree of complexity, the front is that portion of it which contains its main organs of perception and which arrives first whenever it moves in its most characteristic manner of movement. This double criterion for frontness in animate beings may lead to some uncertainties. I assume that for animals, the location of the main organs of perception outweighs the direction-of-movement criterion, since we speak of crabs as moving sideways, not as having heads on one side of their bodies; and since if we found a race of people who typically get around in the way we see people move in reverse motion pictures, I believe we would say of them that they walk backwards rather than that they have faces on the backs of their heads.

Artifacts, or other non-living objects which living beings in some way use or have access to, can also sometimes be said to have fronts and backs. If the object has some surface similarity to a front/back oriented animal,[11] the portion of the object designated as its front is so designated on analogy with the model. Objects which have a fixed orientation when they are in motion have that part which arrives earlier designated as the front. Otherwise, that portion of an object is designated its front if it is that part to which its users are oriented when they are using the object in the principal way which it was intended to be used, or that part of an object is designated as its front if it is the part of the object to which its users typically or importantly or symbolically have access. Notice, incidentally, how the user-orientation criterion and the access criterion operate differently in the case of a traditionally designed church; the user-orientation criterion designates one end of the building as its front, while the access criterion designates the opposite end as its front. One end of the church is thought of as its front on the inside, the opposite end on the outside.

As with "top" and "bottom", the words "front" and "back" designate

---

11. Actually human beings seem to provide the model for these words in English. In the usage by which the "back" of a vertebrate is the surface closest to the spinal column, to most animals the "back" is on top. Use of the word "rear" in these contexts, fairly rare in talk about the locations of objects, would have made the picture simpler.

both extremities and extreme parts of objects or spaces; but unlike "top" and "bottom" they also occur in expressions indicating position outside the object along the front/back axis of the object; in this way they have functions analogous to those of "above" and "below", except that here the setting of the axis is determined by the reference object itself. If an object that we wish to locate is outside the reference object, along the front/back line, and closer to its front extremity, we say it is "in front of" the reference object; if it is outside the reference object but closer to the back extremity, we say it is "in back of" or "behind" the reference object. If the object being located is in contact with the front surface, we say it is "on the front" of it; if it is in contact with the back surface, we say it is "on the back" of it. On the other hand, if it is inside the reference object, the expressions used for indicating whether the object being identified is closer to the front or to the back extremity are, respectively, "in the front" or "in the back" of the reference object. Thus, going back to church, if I ask you to meet me "in back of the church", we will meet outside of the church at one end of the building, but if I ask you to meet me "in the back of the church", we will meet on the inside and at the opposite end. We see then that the words "back" and "front" have uses inside grammaticalized phrases, since "in back of" and "in front of" are perhaps best seen as complex spatial prepositions.[12]

I said earlier that objects which enjoy both an up/down orientation and a front/back orientation also have "sides", known in English as the "left" side and the "right" side. There is a basic sense of the terms "left" and "right" by which human beings are taught to find left and right on their own bodies, and it is likely that this can be learned only by demonstration. There are no simpler concepts in terms of which the notions "left" and "right" can be explicated. Lexicographers have tried various devices for communicating the notions "left" and "right". These devices are usually successful, of course, but what they offer should not be called "definitions" strictly speaking.

---

12. Perhaps it should be noted that "in back of", common in the U.S., does not exist in standard British English, where only "behind" is used.

English language dictionaries typically define "left" as "that side of the body on which in man the muscular action of the limbs is, with most individuals, weaker than on the other side." In the conceptual analysis sense of definition, of course, that is not a *definition* of "left". It is simply not true that "left" and "right" are statistical concepts related to physical strength, and we can be quite sure that speakers of English will continue to use these words in the same way even if it should ever happen that through mutation or exercise, the typical laterality preferences of human beings get reversed. Some dictionaries define "left" as that part of the human body which contains the heart, some as that part of a person which faces west when the person faces north. A Chinese dictionary defines "left" as the opposite of right, and "right" as the opposite of "left". The notions "left" and "right" can be learned, as I suggested, only by demonstration; and, in fact, not everybody succeeds in learning the distinction.

I said that for an object to have left and right sides it is important that it have both a top and a bottom, and a front and a back. A missile traveling in outer space has a front and back, determined by the direction of motion, but in outer space there is no standard reference plane in terms of which it can be said to have an up/down orientation. Accordingly it makes no sense to speak of it having a left and right side, or to speak of it as suddenly taking a turn to the right. An S-shaped loveseat, to take another case, is an object which has a top and a bottom, but no front and back. Accordingly, the arms of a love seat cannot generally be referred to as its left and right arms.

The orientations left and right are fixed first of all for human beings, and then by analogy to other sorts of objects which have the requisite up/down and front/back orientation. For animals or objects which have some surface similarity to humans, left and right are determined by completing the analogy. Can we also know the left and right sides of appliances and vehicles and buildings and furniture just by completing the analogy, that is, by centering our own top-bottom-front-back framework into them and identify their lefts and rights only by knowing top from bottom and front from back? The choice seems to depend on the way in which human beings position themselves with respect to objects. The left drawers of a chest of drawers are to one's left as one confronts the thing; the left arm of a chair or a sofa is to one's right as one faces it. Things with respect to which people orient themselves in opposing ways have left and right undetermined, or determined by an ad hoc convention. Thus the "sinister" and "dexter" portions of an escutcheon are defined in heraldry as the left and right sides from the point of view of the bearer, not the viewer. The expressions "stage left" and "stage right" are the left hand and the right hand parts of the stage from the point of view of the performers, not the audience.

Digression:[13] Consider for a moment the way we talk about flounders. In their deep structure flounders are vertically swimming fish, each equipped with a rotation variable marked plus or minus left. A maturing flounder marked alpha-left undergoes two transformations, one by which it starts swimming on its alpha-left side, another by which its alpha-left eye migrates over its head to the minus-alpha-left side of its head. What in the surface structure of a mature flounder is its top corresponds to the left or right side in the deep structure; in fact, our choice of the words "top" and "bottom" are determined by the surface structure, "left side" and "right side" by the deep structure. The summer flounder swims on its left side, the winter flounder swims on its right side (or else the other way around). We can say of the summer flounder that its top is its right side and its bottom is its left side.

Still another digression: Walking "widdershins" around something is walking around it with one's left side toward it, and walking "deasil" around something is walking around it with one's right side toward it.[14] Sometimes it is explained that these words refer to movement

---

13. The bit here about deep structure, surface structure, transformations, and alpha-variables was supposed to be playful. It appears that some flounders are genetically destined to have their eyes rotate to the left side of their heads, others to the right side. There's no reason this digression needs to stay, except that it once again shows that left/right and top/bottom are not necessarily linked in creatures for which there may be multiple criteria for assigning coordinates.

14. Doubting readers will need to turn to an unabridged dictionary to verify this. I

against or in the direction of the sun's shadows. One way of testing the real meaning of these words is to ship a native speaker of English to the southern hemisphere and to ask him to walk widdershins or deasil around some tree, and see what he does. This will determine whether "left" can be defined as the direction you turn when you walk widdershins in the northern hemisphere or whether "widdershins" needs to have the concept "left" in its definition. One wonders why such a simple experiment has never been tried.

The extremities of the left/right axis of an object are called "sides". Although the word "side" can technically be used of the top side or the back side of an object, the most typical use of the word depends upon an understanding of the particular way in which a physical object is viewed as oriented in space. To see what I mean, consider a large cube that is not intended to be oriented in space in any particular way. When people are asked how many sides that cube has, they typically answer six. Now put that same cube in the middle of a living room, use it as a piece of furniture, with the part that is resting on the floor designated as its bottom and the part that holds the cheese tray and the cocktail glasses designated as the top. How how many sides does it have? It has four sides. Next move it into the baby's room, paint a face on one of its vertical surfaces and pin a tail on the opposite one. Now it has two sides. The English word "side", it appears, is used to designate any smooth face of an object which has not been designated as a top or bottom or as a front or back.

Physical objects have extent in space, the extent of one object can be compared with the extent of another object, and standard-magnitude objects can be taken as units of measure. When measurement becomes abstract, estimates can be made of the distance between two points in space as well as the extent of objects. In a number of cultures, determining the magnitude of manipulable objects is one thing, estimating the distance between two locations, like two villages, involves totally

---

don't now remember (1996) how I first encountered "widdershins"; the word "deasil" I first learned about from Murray Emeneau.

different concepts. According to Hallowell (1957),[15] the Saulteaux Indians measure walls, canoes, or tools, with fathoms, cubits, or finger-stretches, but it is not even conceivable to them that the distance between two towns can be indicated in comparable terms. Longer distances, that is, are always measured in terms of the amount of time it takes to get from one of them to the other. If the two towns are at a distance that cannot be traveled in one day, they are, say, "three sleeps apart". Shorter distances are indicated by pointing to the extent of the sky that the sun travels in the time it takes to get from one town to the other.

Consider some of the words we use in English for speaking about the measurement of objects and the distance between places. Consider, first, an object which has one of its dimensions considerably greater than the others. If this object has no vertical orientation, we say that it is "long" or "short", or we say that it is "so many units long". If, on the other hand, the object is vertically oriented along one of its major dimensions, we say that it is "tall" or "short", depending on how it compares with the norm we have in mind, or that it is so many measurement units "tall". For distances, we say that an object is "far from" or "near to" a mentioned or unmentioned reference object if the two locations are not seen as being generally on the same vertical axis, but we say that something is "high" or "low" if what we are concerned with is its vertical distance from the horizon or the earth's surface or some other reference point.

In expressing measurement of objects that are viewed as having a spatial orientation, the adjectives that accompany these measurement indications are selected according to a number of assumptions we make about the salient dimensions and the specific spatial orientation of the objects in question. The linguist who has had the most to say about the features that I am about to describe is Manfred Bierwisch

15. A. Irving Hallowell, *Culture and Experience* (Pennsylvania: University of Pennsylvania Press, 1957) Chapter 10.

(1967).[16] Bierwisch's examples were from German, and German and English measurement adjectives have some interesting differences, but I will speak of the English equivalents. Consider first the way in which the word "wide" is used in measurement expressions for roughly oblong objects. Suppose there is a plot of land 75 feet by 200 feet in dimension out in the middle of nowhere, and you ask somebody to go out and measure it and to report to you the results of his measurements. He will probably come back and tell you that the lot is 75 feet wide and 200 feet long. Now build a road along the 200 foot length of this lot in a way to suggest that this is a lot that has one of its borders along a road in some future housing development, and ask somebody to go out and measure the lot. This time you will be told that the lot is 200 feet wide and 75 feet deep. Putting the road alongside of the lot will have served to designate one border of that lot as its "front", and when an object to be measured has a front/back orientation in space, the word "wide" is used in measuring the left-to-right extent along its front, and the word used for indicating the measurement of its front-to-back distance is the word "deep". This is true of three-dimensional objects as well as areas of land, so that, for example, a table that measures three feet by five feet will be described as three feet wide and five feet long, while a desk having the same dimensions will be described as five feet wide and three feet deep.

The word "deep" has a second use as well. Where the "salient" or "base line" extremity along the top/bottom axis of an object is its bottom, we say that the object is so many units "high" or "tall" (depending on certain shape criteria), but where the base line vertical extremity is the top of an object, we speak of its top-to-bottom dimension as being so many units "deep". A building is "high" or "tall", a pond or well is "deep". For certain kinds of objects it is uncertain what the base line is, and so we don't know whether it's "high" or "deep". One example is a

---

16. See his "Some Semantic Universals of German Adjectivals," *Foundations of Language* 3.1 (1967).

drawer. Some people will describe the top-to-bottom dimension of a drawer as its height, others as its depth. To these latter, the question "How deep is your desk drawer?" is ambiguous because one could be speaking about the measurement from its top to its bottom, or the distance from front to back. The word "deep", then, has these two functions. (There is a third, too, which I will only mention in passing. Something is said to be "deep in x" if x can be a large bounded area and the location is far from the boundary, as in "deep in the forest".) In any case, the word "deep" is appropriate only if what is measured is the dimension of an enclosure.

In Bierwisch's terms, the adjectives "high", "long", "wide", and "deep" are used only for indicating measurements along salient dimensions. Where a dimension is not salient, the adjective needed is "thick". To give some of Bierwisch's examples, a *board* has two "salient" dimensions, and if one of these is greater than the other, we say that the board is wide, long and thick by so many units each, the dimension indicated as "thick" being nonsalient. A *door* has a left-to-right dimension or a width, a top-to-bottom dimension or a height, and one nonsalient dimension, its thickness. While a board is long, wide and thick, a door is high, wide, and thick. A *drawer* has a left-to-right dimension, its width, a top-to-bottom dimension, its height, and a salient front-to-back dimension, its depth. A drawer, on the German pattern at least, is high, wide, and deep. The word "deep" is used for the front-to-back distance of an area or of a stationary storage object; for an object which moves, on the other hand, the front-to-back distance is its length. Thus an *automobile* has a left-to-right dimension, its width, a top-to-bottom dimension, its height, and a front-to-back dimension, its length. Reviewing: an automobile is long, wide, and high; a drawer is high, wide, and deep; a door is high, wide, and thick; and a board is long, wide, and thick.

So far I have mentioned only static concepts associated with space. Many spatial notions are associated with movement, and it is to that that I would like to turn now. The kind of movement that will concern me has to do with "locomotion": an object changing its location through time. In characterizing an instance of locomotion, we can indicate the position of the object at an earlier point in time, the position of the object at a later point in time, and we can in some way characterize the path that connects these two locations. If we follow the tradition of identifying the point of origin as the Source and the destination as the Goal, and if we consider the dimensionality distinctions that I mentioned earlier, we can see, as has been pointed out many times, that the three-way distinction which we found for expressions of simple location involving English prepositions, namely expressions with "at", "on", and "in", are paralleled with Source and Goal expressions too. If we take x as the point of origin of movement, then "from x", "off of x", and "out of x" are the three Source expressions which impute to x, respectively, no particular dimensionality, the property of being or having a surface, and the property of being or having an interior. Paralleling these distinctions in Goal-of-motion phrases we find "to x", "onto x", and "into x". David Bennett has pointed out (Bennett 1970/72)[17] that when the Path of a movement is indicated by a salient intermediate location, the three-way dimensionality distinction holds there, too. "Via", Bennett claims, is the path-indicating preposition with no presuppositions about the dimensionality of the object named by the following noun; "over" and "through" are the prepositions that have associated with them notions of surface and interiority respectively.

The case-like notions that we have need of for descriptions of instances of locomotion, then, all seem to require an understanding of the same dimensionality distinctions which we found necessary for expressions of simple location. One might very well wish to take the prepositions of Location, Source, Path, and Goal, which have no dimensionality presuppositions associated with them, and regard them as expressing the basic static and dynamic positional notions; and regard all such other notions as surface, interior, front, back, top, bottom, etc., as belonging to a separate system of semantic concepts

17. David C. Bennett, Some Observations Concerning the Locative-Directional Distinction, *Semiotica* 5: 109–127. I was referring to a mimeographed draft dated 1970.

associated with the space-semantics of words naming locations and objects. Taking this point of view, we can regard the locational and directional notions associated with "at", "from", "via", and "to", as being basic, regarding all other locative or directional concepts as being conceptually more complex. By this analysis, "in x", for example, is to be analyzed as meaning "at a place which is inside x"; "into x" can be analyzed as "to a place which is inside x"; "through x" can be analyzed as "via a place which is inside x"; and "out of x" can be analyzed as "from a place which is inside x". Something like this is essentially what Jeffrey Gruber (1965),[18] Geoffrey Leech (1975) [fn. 9], and David Bennett (1975)[19] have proposed.

There are in English many directional complements of the preposition phrase type which have the same form as the underlying locative complement. This is true of the complements of the *Path* and *Goal* type, but it is not true of *Source* complements, because it seems that Source complements are essentially always marked with a Source-indicating preposition. An expression like "behind the sofa" can appear in a purely Locative expression, as in "He left his slippers behind the sofa"; it can occur as a Goal expression, as in "The cat ran behind the sofa"; it can occur as a Path expression, as in "The cat ran behind the sofa and out the window."

Our examples with "behind" showed that there are Goal complements which have the same form as the corresponding Locative expression. The next thing to consider is the case of a Locative expression which has the form of a Goal or Path expression. The function of these expressions is that of indicating the location of an object by making use of two reference objects, one of them possibly implicit. A way of looking at these expressions is that they indicate the location of objects as the destination of possible journeys or movements. Thus, if I say "The cemetery is beyond the chapel from the post office," you can think of

---

18. Jeffrey Gruber, *Studies in Lexical Relations*, MIT Dissertation (1965).

19. David C. Bennett, *Spatial and Temporal Uses of English Prepositions: An Essay in Stratificational Semantics* (London: Longman, 1975).

the location of the cemetery as the destination of a journey, a more or less straight-line journey to be sure, which began at the post office and went past the chapel. Similarly, if I said "Fred lives past the cemetery," one might interpret what I have said as meaning that if one makes a straight-line journey from some implicit starting point and goes via the cemetery, one will come to Fred's house.

The notion of a straight-line journey, which I called on for explaining the locative use of directional phrases, presupposes an understanding of maintaining a constant direction. The most typical way of maintaining a constant direction involves having standard orientation points provided for the users of the language by physical features of the environment. In many communities the points of the compass are used for this, of course, but in localities that have particularly noticeable physical features that do not orient themselves by the compass, terms that refer to these features take on a greater importance in indicating direction of movement than the cardinal directions themselves. That this can be so even in an English-speaking community will be obvious to anyone who has tried to read a newspaper in Honolulu.

Digression: To the extent that standard orientation points have great social or mythic importance in the community, the participants in the culture experience distress whenever they are not sure of their location with respect to these orientation points. This is the experience of being *disoriented*, and I assume that it should be of greater interest to a psychologist than to a linguist, but it might be interesting to remark that, according to Hallowell, the Ojibwa Indians experienced distress when they lost track of their orientation in space, but had no particular concern about what day it was. A Euro-American, by comparison, can become quite uncomfortable if he does not know whether it is Tuesday or Sunday, but can live happily for days on end without ever knowing whether he is facing north or south.

In this lecture I have reviewed a number of the concepts involving space which have some relevance to semantic and pragmatic facts about the vocabulary of natural languages. In my next lecture I will do the same for concepts of time. In some ways, time is conceptually simpler than space, since it only has one dimension and is unidirectional. But there are complications enough there too, as you will see.

In my second lecture I spoke about non-deictic conceptions of space; today I will be talking about non-deictic conceptions of time. I will unfortunately have nothing to say about the mysteries and paradoxes of time, the perception of time, illusions about the passing of time which people in different psychological states are said to experience, or indeed any of the really interesting and important insights about time which physicists, astronauts, theologians, and acidheads are said to possess. I'll only talk about a few of the simpler temporal concepts, just a few among those that we need to be able to refer to when we talk about the meanings of lexical items or the functions of grammatical categories in natural languages.

The first thing to notice about time is that it is one-dimensional and unidirectional. If two events can be said to take place at different moments of time, it is necessarily the case that one of them is *earlier*, the other *later*. Since time is unidirectional, the relationship between that which remains the same at different times and the time dimension itself is frequently thought of by the human mind as *movement*. The movement metaphor for time allows one to think of "the world" as moving through time, or "the world" as being constant and time passing by it.

I said earlier in connection with the front/back orientation of objects in motion that the "front" of a moving object was that part of the object which arrives at places earlier than the rest. For things which are located outside a front/back oriented object and are situated along the front/back axis, we say that they are "in front of" or "in back of" that object depending on whether they are closer to the front or the rear of the object. Another way of saying "in back of" is "behind". What I did not point out before is that just in case the setting of the front/back orientation of an object is determined by whether the object is in motion, another way of saying "in front of" is "ahead". In the movement metaphor for time, the front/back axis is set one way or the other depending on whether we regard time as stable and the continuing world as being in motion, or whether the continuing world is taken as the stable reference point and time is thought of as being in motion. Some locutions in English take the metaphor one way, others take it the other way. In a sentence like "Success lay behind them, failure lay ahead of them," the words "ahead" and "behind" identify periods that are later and earlier respectively than the reference time of the sentence. In a sentence like "Before that time they were successful, after that time they were unsuccessful," the words "before" and "after", derived from expressions relating to spatial orientation, are historically based on the moving-time metaphor. If it is time that is moving, the part that has gone by is leading, is ahead, and the part that is yet to come is lagging behind; if it is the human world that is moving with respect to time, the part that has not yet been experienced is ahead of the travellers, the part that has been experienced already is behind. Different languages arrange the metaphors differently for different uses, and sometimes, as we see in English, the same language can use both metaphors in related expressions. To take another example of the distinction in English, consider expressions like "in the months ahead" as opposed to expressions like "in the following months". The two expressions mean the same thing, but one puts later time ahead, the other puts later time behind.

The words "earlier" and "later", by contrast, are basic temporal notions, not based on a movement metaphor. In fact, an understanding of the setting of the front/back axis for an object in motion presupposed an understanding of unidirectional time, since "front" was defined in that case in terms of a part of something "arriving earlier" than the rest of it.

We can talk about events occurring in time, we can say that one event occured earlier in time than another, and we can talk about events having duration in time. The extent of time during which an event occurs, or, in fact, an extent of time defined in any way whatever, can be thought of as having a beginning and an end, these unambiguously identified as the earliest and latest time points at which the events can be said to be going on.

Notice the proportionality between "beginning" and "end" with "top" and "bottom" and with "front" and "back", and the proportionality of "before" and "after" with "above" and "below" and with "ahead" and "behind." The up/down orientation provides an axis along which we can speak of the location of objects with respect to a given reference object. If the object being located is outside of the reference object but along the axis, we speak of it as being "above" or "below" the object. If it is an extremity or a part of the reference object located at one of the extremities along the up/down axis as defined by the typical or symbolic orientation of the object, we use the words "top" and "bottom". Similarly with the front/back axis. The nouns "front" and "back" indicate portions of the reference object, the phrases "in front of" and "in back of"–without the definite article–or the words "ahead" and "behind", indicate position outside of the reference object but along the front/back axis. The temporal axis is set up by the earlier/later relationship between events. A time period has an extent along this axis, and "locations" in time can be thought of as positioned with respect to a given time period along the temporal axis. The position of a time period outside the reference period calls for the prepositions "before" and "after", the earlier and later extremities of the reference period being indicated by the words "beginning" and "end". And like the words "front" and "back" and "top" and "bottom", the words "beginning" and "end" can be used either for naming *extremities* or *portions* of the time period.

Digression: Notice that the various axes have certain inherent differences, making it always possible for us to keep them apart conceptually. The up/down axis is determined by the direction of the pull of gravitational forces, and the outside-the-reference-object indicators "above" and "below" are unambiguously specifiable independently of whether the reference object itself has an up/down orientation or whether the up/down axis defined for the object is set to agree with the gravitational up/down axis. (I can be under something even if it's upside down.) The setting of the front/back axis is determined by the built-in orientational properties of the object itself, as defined by the various criteria I mentioned last time, or by the direction of movement. I can therefore be in front of somebody when he faces me but in back of him the next moment if he turns around. With the temporal axis, however, the earlier/later orientation is permanently set, and the beginning and end portions of a time period are not conceivable independently of the earlier/later ordering relation in time.

We recognize time periods and time points, and we recognize that a time period can be defined uniquely by identifying its beginning and ending time points. Time periods can be compared with one another, so that we can speak of one time period being longer or shorter than another. The activities of human beings establish various norms for time periods, and the vocabulary of a language can have words that name relatively short periods like "a while", very short periods like "moment", "jiffy", and "trice"; very long periods like "eon", "age", and "era"; or a maximally long period like "eternity".

In addition to speaking of events occurring in time and occupying time periods, we can speak of event types *recurring* in time. Certain *ordinal time specifiers* indicate recurrences of event types, as in a sentence like "John went to Chicago *twice* last month." The same event type—that is, two events of the same type – occurred at two different times.

When nature provides sequentially recurring event types having apparently the same duration, these event types can be used to provide measuring units for temporal extent. The recurring event types that are most constant, most common, and most accessible to ordinary observers are the daily alternation of light and dark, changes in how the moon looks to us, and the apparent annual course of the sun accompanied by the regularly recurring changes in the seasons. These particular event types are cycles which do not involve the sequencing of discrete separable events, and so, when they are used for providing units of measure, it is necessary to identify recurrences of the *same phase* of the cycle. Those phases which seem to have constant temporal extents between recurrences of them are, for example, the full moon, the most vertical position of the sun, the shortest day of the year, etc.

If these cycles are to be taken only as units of measure, it makes no difference which phase of the cycle is taken as the starting point for the measurement; one cycle has passed with the return to the same phase. If, however, these cyclic events are to provide concepts for locating events in "absolute time", then there is a special need for *fixed-phase* units, time units which have been assigned fixed starting points recognizable, in principle, by all members of the speech community.

Time measure periods taken only as units of measure we can call *non-calendric*. Time measure periods having fixed starting points in absolute time can be called *calendric*. Many of the time measure words in English have both calendric and noncalendric uses, for example, the word "year". If I say that the time between noon on June 28, 1971 and noon on June 28, 1972 is one year, I am using the word "year" non-calendrically. On the other hand, if I use the expression "last year", meaning the period of time between the beginning of January 1, 1970 and the end of December 31, 1970, I am using the word "year" in its calendric sense.

In addition to the time units which are provided more or less directly by the phenomena of nature, it is possible for the members of a human community to construct derivative units consisting of *partitions* of the naturally given time units, or *sequences* of the natural units. The day is divided into 24 hours, each hour into 60 minutes, each minute into 60 seconds, and so on. Specialists make even further divisions. These terms are used mainly as non-calendric or pure measurement units, but for "hour", at least in communities where class lectures or radio programs are scheduled in hour-long blocks of time matching clock time, it has a calendric use, too. A disc jockey, for example, can speak of ending one hour with a commercial and beginning the next hour with the news.

Examples of derivative units defined as fixed-length sequences of naturally given time units include "week", "fortnight", "pentad", "decade", "century", etc. The word "week" can be taken as either a calendric or a noncalendric unit, the word "fortnight" has only a non-calendric use.

In addition to these more or less explicitly bounded time periods, there are other sequences which are informal and vague with respect to their boundaries, but which relate in some way to local "outdoor" changes. The annual cycle, for example, is divisible into "seasons", and the daily cycle is divided into the parts of the day such as "morning", "afternoon", "evening", and "night". In some languages, the long period we call "night" has many subdivisions, and some languages have more or fewer distinctions than we have for the daylight hours.

The seasons and the subdivisions of the day are informal units, though, as we know, in communities which support astronomers and clock-makers, the separate seasons are taken as having fixed starting points. Even at that, their informal character is not lost, however, as we know when we hear our Michigan friends complain about having a long winter. That the terms have more to do with what it's like outside than with parts of the calendar year is clear from the fact that the cycle is shifted by two seasons in the southern hemisphere, and that in many parts of the world we are told that they lack the standard four seasons, and use some other number, such as two, for example, "wet" and "dry".

The calendric "day" can be used to refer to a recurring 24-hour cycle, conventionally recycling at midnight, or it can refer just to the daylight portion of the cycle, in opposition to "night". The word "morning" can be used to refer to the daylight hours before noon, or to that part of the calendar day before noon. Thus, the "morning" is that part of the "day" which ends at noon, in either of the two calendric senses of "day". Next time you hear somebody say, "Why are you calling me in the middle of the night? Don't you realize it's three o'clock in the morning?" point out to him that he has chosen the word "night" from the day-subdivision cycle which is not put in phase with the calendar day and that he has chosen the word "morning" from the day-subdivision cycle which is put in phase with the calendar day, and explain to him that the reason is that only the latter is appropriate in expressions of clock time.

Some repeating sequences have named members, as, for example, the sequence "morning"/"afternoon"/"evening"/"night", the sequence "summer"/"autumn"/"winter"/"spring", the sequence "Sunday"/ "Monday", etc., and two that I haven't mentioned yet, namely, the months of the year and the numbered dates of months. The named members of cycles I will refer to as *positional* terms.

Some of the positional term sequences have *designated first members*, while others do not. The reason for the difference seems to be that cycles can be said to have fixed starting points only if they are run through completely within some larger time unit, with their first member beginning at the same time the larger unit begins. As it happens, there is a calendar year change during the winter and a calendar day change during the night. Since the annual cycle of seasons is does not begin and end with the calendar year, and since the day-subdivision cycle does not begin and end with the calendar day, these two cycles do not have first members.

A formally defined cycle, such as that comprising the names of the days of the week, can quite easily have a "first" member, since the word "week" designates this seven-member sequence by definition. However, there is one fussy and unfortunate problem with that, and that is that people do not agree on which is the first day of the week. Calendar makers typically start the week off with Sunday, but ever since the beginning of the five-day work week, many people speak of Monday as the first day of the week. This difference will take on some importance when we talk later about deictic calendric expressions.

The annual solar cycle and the lunar cycle are not in phase naturally, so in communities which make use of the lunar calendar but recognize the annual cycle with some accuracy, there is typically no first month. In the lunar calendar used by the Saulteaux, the months are named by the animals or plants which first make their appearance during that month. (Again, my source is Hallowell.) Since the Saulteaux have no fixed-phase calendar year which exactly includes the complete sequence of the lunations, there is no first month. Accordingly, when the Saulteaux are asked to recite the names of the months, they recite them in order, beginning with the current month. (Incidentally, when the lunar calendar gets out of phase with the biological year, the Saulteaux just let one month go by unnamed.)

The months of our calendar have their origin in the lunar calendar, but they are now artificial segments of the calendar year. The word "month" has both a calendric and a non-calendric use, but because of the differing lengths of different months, it does not name a constant length unit in either of these senses. The problem becomes apparent if you move into an apartment on the 18th of the month and you have signed a three-month lease; you will be expected to leave by the 17th of the month three months later, no matter how long the intervening months are. (Bankers, of course, use the word more carefully. A three-month loan must be paid off in 90 days.)

Summarizing, cyclically recurring events provide standard measurement units for time periods. Non-calendric terms are used only for measuring time intervals. When designated phases of cycles are taken as fixed starting points, the word used to indicate the period between one such phase and the next is a calendric term. Derivative non-calendric and calendric units are defined as segments or sequences of the naturally given units. Some calendric units are the named members of larger cycles. These I call *positional*, because they indicate a position within a sequence. Positional calendric units, then, include "April", "Tuesday", "morning", and "winter". There is a difference between positional-term sequences that are put in phase with larger calendric units and those which are not. The names of the seasons are not put in phase with the calendar year. The names of the day-subdivisions have one use by which they are and another use by which they are not. In one usage, the night ends at the same moment the day ends (midnight), and the morning and the day begin at that same moment; in the other usage, the day cycle changes at midnight, but the transition from night to morning is at sunrise. The day names and the month names, by virtue of being artificial or "culturally" imposed units, are put in phase with higher calendric units, namely the calendar week and the calendar year respectively. All of these distinctions will become important later, when we talk about deictic time expressions.

So far, now, we are equipped to talk about priority in time, extent in time, cycles which allow measurement of temporal extents, and the *phase-fixing* of these cycles. In order to locate events unambiguously in "absolute time", it is necessary to have one or more absolute temporal reference points, and for that a community can choose something like the presumed birth date of a culture hero, the beginning of a revolution, an emperor's accession to the throne, and so on. Once a temporal reference point has been established, it is then possible to speak of any point in time as being at a measurable distance earlier or later than, or coinciding with the accepted reference point. Notice that I am now talking about an objective, external temporal reference point in "absolute time". In contrast to this, when we talk about deictic time expressions, we will make use of a subjective, changing temporal reference point, namely the moment of speaking, the coding time.

We can talk about a time point or a time period, we are able to locate the time point or the beqinning and end of a time period at a particular "location" in "absolute time", if we care to, and we are able to indicate the length, or *duration*, of a span of time. The phrase which associates the time of an event with that event might not specify the exact moment, but might specify instead a larger calendar-unit which includes the time of the event. A sentence like "He was born in 1940" can be thought of as elliptical for "at a time which is included in 1940".

There are a great many devices for indicating the relative times of two-events—that is, devices for identifying the time of one event relative to the time of another event. Some of these have to do with time units of the sort we have been discussing. Thus, if I say "She divorced Schwartz and married Harry in the same week," I have located two events as occurring within a single calendar week; but if I say "She divorced Schwartz and married Harry within a week," I have located the two events as having occurred within a single seven-day stretch, but this time the two points are free to cross the boundaries of the calendar week. Similarly, if I say that one thing happened "a week later" than another, I say that there is a seven-day-long span between the two events; if I say the one thing happened "the next week" after the other, I say that the two events happened in two successive calendar weeks, but I haven't said whether the time between the two events is three or six or ten days.

In general, though there is apparently a certain amount of dialect variation here, there is a systematic difference in the understanding of *positional* terms depending on the presence or absence of a *demonstrative*, and in the understanding of *nonpositional* terms depending on whether a *definite or indefinite determiner* is used, as is shown in the following examples: "He was to meet her on Thursday" means that he was scheduled to meet her on the first Thursday after the reference time; "He was to meet her that Thursday," by contrast, adds the understanding that the reference time itself was within the same calendar week as the Thursday in question. Similarly with "He had arrived in London on Thursday" as compared with "He had arrived in London that Thursday." The former sentence could be spoken on Monday, the latter could not. In the sentences about remarriage in the preceding paragraph, there would be a difference between "within a week", which has the interpretation I gave it, and "within the week", which means the same thing as "within the same week." It should follow, and I think it does, that terms which have no calendric function do not occur with the definite article: thus, we can say "in a while" but not "in the while", "within a fortnight", but not "within the fortnight", "in a trice", but not "in the trice", and so on. These remarks, needless to say, are to be taken with the usual qualifications one adds to generalizations about the use of English articles.

Expressions not identifying calendar units can indicate relations of *priority, coincidence,* or *containment* between the times of two events. Coincidence can be made explicit with expressions like "at the same time" or "simultaneously" or less explicit with a "when"-clause. Near coincidence, or close succession, can be indicated with an expression like "as soon as". Containment of a point within a span can be expressed as in "She was watching *Sesame Street* when I left"; containment of a span within a span can be expressed as in "I read *War and Peace* while she talked to her mother on the phone." And so on. Priority in time can be shown with "before" and "after," and these are paraphrasable as "at a time which is earlier than the time when" and "at a time which is later than the time when", respectively.

Digression: We must keep in mind the difference between the *factive* and the *counterfactive* uses of "before." Its factive use is seen in "He finished the symphony before he died," where the clause that follows "before" is assumed to be true; its counterfactive use is seen in "He died before he finished the symphony." The difference can be made apparent when we try to introduce a temporal extent phrase. "He finished the symphony three days before he died" is okay, but "He died three days before he finished the symphony" is not. A sentence like "He got sick before he finished the symphony" is ambiguous, then, in a way in which "He got sick three days before he finished the symphony" is not.

There are various verbs in our language which make it possible to relate an event to an indication of the extent of time during which the event can be said to have occurred. One example is the verb "last." The noun "concert" is the name of an occasion or event which has a temporal extent, and we can say such things as "The concert lasted three hours." There are also verbs which relate the agent in an event to the event and to the time span occupied by the event. Some event types are characterized as having fixed terminations, others are characterized in terms of the activity itself. We can call these *bounded* and *unbounded*, and refer to the verbs as *completive* and *durative*, respectively. Time-indicating verbs of the type I have been discussing which distinguish between these two notions are the verbs "take" and "spend". Notice that we can say "It took me three hours to *find* the diamond" and "I spent three hours *looking for* the diamond." Verbs like "look for" and "find" have the aspectual information built in, but certain verbs can be used in either way. Thus, in "It took me three hours to read the book," the verb "read" is understood completively whereas with a sentence like "I spent three hours reading the book," there is no suggestion that I finished reading it.

Digression: the time extent *preposition-phrases* are selected according to this same distinction. Notice the difference between "I read the book in three hours" and "I read the book for three hours"; notice too that "I looked for the diamond for three hours" is better than "I looked for the diamond in three hours," and "I found the diamond in three hours" is better than "I found the diamond for three hours."

The verbs "last", "take", and "spend" are verbs which in different ways indicate something about the relation between an event and the temporal extent of that event. All three of these verbs can have their temporal extent complements given as either calendric or non-calendric units. For example, one can say "The concert lasted all afternoon" or "I spent Sunday looking for the diamond" as well as one can use pure measurement phrases like the "three hours" of my earlier examples. There is another verb which is used to indicate the distance in time between two reference points in time, and that is the verb "elapse". This verb accepts as its temporal expression only a non-calendric time extent phrase. For example, although it is possible to say "Two days elapsed", it is not possible to say "Monday and Tuesday elapsed."

I said earlier that since the time dimension is unidirectional, there are fixed earliest and latest time points within any span of time. A time period can be indicated not only by means of a measurement expression, but also by identifying one or both of the extremities of the period. The prepositions which indicate the early and late extremities are "from" and "until," as seen in "The concert lasted from noon until midnight." There are analogies between time-extent expressions and the source/goal/distance notions associated with movement in space, and in many cases similar syntax is called for. We say both "He stayed there from Monday to Friday" and "He travelled from Chicago to Pittsburgh." In the temporal "movement" case, however, there is nothing that corresponds to the notion Path which we proposed for characterizing movement in space. There is only one route between two time points: one cannot go from 1970 to 1971 by passing through 1929.

In addition to the notions of the actual time of an event, one can also speak about the expected or theoretical time of an event. That being so, we can talk about the difference between the actual time and the expected time, as in sentences like "John arrived early" or "John arrived late." One can furthermore talk about an agent in an event doing something in order that the actual time of the event will be different from the expected time. The verb "postpone" refers to doing something so that the beginning of the event will be later than the time expected for the event to begin, and the verb "prolong" refers to doing something which will cause the end of the time period for an event to be later than what was expected. And so on.

When we think about *tenses*, the first words which come to mind are "past", "present", and "future." These are notions related to deictic time, and that is something that will concern us shortly. The notions associated with tense that can be taken up in connection with nondeictic time are, in particular, the difference between the time of an event or a condition—let's call it the *event time*—and the time or time period that is taken as the background or setting for time indications in the clause—and let's call that the *reference time*. The simplest illustration of this distinction is the so-called *perfect* construction, seen most clearly in one use of the past perfect, as in "John had retired three years earlier." Here, the reference time is associated with the tense on "had" and can be interpreted only by knowing the discourse context of the sentence; the event of John's retiring is placed at three years earlier to the reference time.

In my next lecture I will begin the discussion of *deixis*.

DEIXIS I

In my lecture on the sentence "May we come in?" I spoke about lexical items and grammatical forms which can be interpreted only when the sentences in which they occur are understood as being anchored in some social context, that context defined in such a way as to identify the participants in the communication act, their location in space, and the time during which the communication act is performed. Aspects of language which require this sort of contextualization are what I have been calling *deictic*. In my second and third lectures I spoke about the non-deictic semantics of expressions which serve to locate objects and events in *space* and *time*. Today I will talk about deictic space and time expressions. My next lecture on deixis will cover *social* and *discourse* deixis.

One way to become clear about the importance of deictic anchoring is to consider a variety of cases in which messages can be correctly interpreted only if they are properly anchored in a communication situation, but where there are mistakes or uncertainties about the nature of this anchoring.

Suppose, first, that you are a young lady who has just heard a wolf whistle, and you feel like letting the wolf know that you resent what he did. There are two uncertainties in this situation, one of them being that you can't be sure who emitted the whistle, the second being that you may not have been the addressee of the compliment. To turn around and scowl is to acknowledge that you believe the message was intended for you, and that may be taken as presumptuous. The meaning of the message is fairly clear, but what is uncertain is the identity of the sender and that of the intended receiver.

Here is another case. Suppose that you are looking for somebody in the place where he works, and when you get to his office you find taped to his door a sign which reads "back in two hours". The message is clear, you can probably be pretty sure who the sender of the message was, and you can properly consider yourself included in the set of intended receivers of the message. This time, however, an important bit of information is missing, namely the time at which the message was written.

Consider a third case. Herb Clark has brought to my attention some experiments that were conducted with preschool children communicating with each other across a barrier. They could hear each other, but they could not see each other. Each child had in front of him an array of blocks, and the experiment was to see how well children of different ages could communicate with each other by linguistic means alone. One child was told how to assemble the blocks to make a particular figure, and his job was to teach the child on the other side of the barrier how to do the same thing. It was not uncommon, Clark tells me, for the one child to say, "Put this block on top of that one," for the other then to say, "You mean this one?" and for the first to reply, "Yes."

This is characteristic of what Piaget refers to as the egocentric speech of children under the age of about seven. What is important for us to notice is that the children were using demonstratives in contexts requiring gestures that should have been monitored by their conversation partners, but neither sender nor receiver apparently sensed that need.

Take another case. Suppose this time that you are in a large building whose echoing properties you are not familiar with, and you are trying to locate somebody you believe to be in this building. You call out, "Yoohoo, Jimmy, where are you?" and you hear Jimmy's voice coming from somewhere saying "I'm right here." You know that he is telling the truth, but unless you can tell where his voice is coming from, you still don't know where he is. You call him again, and he says, somewhat impatiently this time, "I'm right here." Eventually you may find him, but in the process you will have learned that the only function of a sentence like "I'm right here" is that of emitting a noise that will somehow help people guess where you are. Counting aloud to three would do just as well.

The worst possible case I can imagine for a totally unanchored occasion-sentence is that of finding afloat in the ocean a bottle containing a note which reads, "Meet me here at noon tomorrow with a stick about this big."

There are many less obvious examples of anchoring mistakes and confusions that one can think of. A sentence like "The farmer killed the duckling," which is the way people usually remember the Sapir sentence I mentioned in my first lecture, can only be properly uttered in a discourse context in which the reference time reflected in the simple past tense of the verb has been identified in the preceding context, as well as the identity of a particular farmer and a particular duckling. People who feel that biblical injunctions ought to be obeyed should pay attention to who the injunctions were addressed to. What they fail to realize is that when the intended addressee of a command complies with the command, the command no longer stands. The biblical command, "Be fruitful and multiply", has been complied with, in spades, and nobody living today can consider himself or herself among the intended receivers of that message. The earth has been replenished and subdued.

Deixis is the name given to those formal properties of utterances which are determined by, and which are interpreted by knowing, certain aspects of the communication act in which the utterances in question can play a role. These include (1) the identity of the interlocutors in a communication situation, covered by the term *person deixis*; (2) the place or places in which these individuals are located, for which we have the term *place deixis*; (3) the time at which the communication act takes place—for this we may need to distinguish as the *encoding time*, the time at which the message is sent, and as the *decoding time*, the time at which the message is received—these together coming under the heading of *time deixis*; (4) the matrix of linguistic material within which the utterance has a role, that is, the preceding and following parts of the discourse, which we can refer to as *discourse deixis*; and (5) the social relationships on the part of the participants in the conversation, that determine, for example, the choice of honorific or polite or intimate or insulting speech levels, etc., which we can group together under the term *social deixis*.

Today, as I said, I will be speaking mainly about place deixis and time deixis; in the final lecture I will have something to say about social deixis and discourse deixis, and I will include remarks on person deixis in my discussion of social deixis. There are certain person deictic categories, however, which are relevant to the description of both place deixis and time deixis, and I will identify these briefly now.

There is, first of all, the speaker of the utterance, the *sender* of the message, what grammarians call the "first person"; there is, secondly, the *addressee* of the message or utterance, the message's intended recipient, what we usually refer to as the "second person"; there is a third category of person deixis which is seldom included in discussions of pronoun systems or person markers in languages, presumably because it seldom has obvious reflexes in the morphology of a language, but which plays a role nevertheless—I have in mind the intended *audience*, by which I mean a person who may be considered part of the conversational group but who is not a member of the speaker/addressee pair. The three categories of person deixis that I will be talking about, then, are *speaker, addressee,* and *audience.* (Out of habit I use the word "speaker" even though I mean "sender".) Other individuals referred to in sentences can be identified negatively with respect to these three categories as being, for example, somebody who is neither speaker nor addressee, or somebody who is neither speaker nor addressee nor audience.

The most obvious place-deictic terms in English are the adverbs "here" and "there" and the demonstratives "this" and "that", along with their plural forms; the most obvious time-deictic words are adverbs like "now" or "today".

There are important distinctions in the uses of these and other deictic words which I would like us to be clear about right away. I will frequently need to point out whether a word or expression that I am referring to can be used in one or more of three different ways, and these I will call *gestural, symbolic,* and *anaphoric.* By the *gestural* use of a deictic expression I mean that use by which it can be properly interpreted only by somebody who is monitoring some physical aspect of the communication situation; by the *symbolic* use of a deictic expression I mean that use whose interpretation involves merely knowing certain aspects of the speech communication situation, whether this knowledge comes by current perception or not; and by the *anaphoric* use of an expression I mean that use which can be correctly interpreted by knowing what other portion of the same discourse the expression is *coreferential* with.

I can illustrate the distinction I'm talking about by taking the word "there". It has all three uses. Its gestural use can be seen in a sentence like, "I want you to put it there." You have to know where the speaker is pointing in order to know what place he is indicating. The symbolic use is exemplified in the telephoner's utterance, "Is Johnny there?" This time we understand the word "there" as meaning "in the place where you are." An example of the anaphoric use of "there" is a sentence like "I drove the car to the parking lot and left it there." In that case the word refers to a place which had been identified earlier in the discourse, namely the parking lot.

Take another example, this time one showing just the distinction between the gestural and the symbolic use. If during my lecture you hear me use a phrase like "this finger", the chances are fairly good that you will look up to see what it is that I want you to see; you will expect the word to be accompanied by a gesture or demonstration of some sort.

On the other hand, if you hear me use the phrase "this campus", you do not need to look up, because you know my meaning to be "the campus in which I am now located", and you happen to know where I am. The former is the gestural use, the latter the symbolic use.

One way to become sensitive in a hurry to the role of deixis-accompanying gestures is to have conversations with blind people, and with deaf people who can read lips. When you are talking with blind people, you detect instantly that gestures which require your interlocutor to see what you are doing are impossible. This is sensed as an inconvenience, but the nature of the problem can be mastered instantly. In conversations with a deaf person who can read lips, the fact that he can see you may cause you to rely on gestures more than you normally would, since gestures are generally an aid to communication. It is easy to forget that your addressee cannot look at what you are pointing at and simultaneously read your lips. If you want to talk about, say, a city on a map, you can point to the map, but then you must wait for him to look back at your lips again before you can resume talking.

There are not very many deictic expressions which function gesturally only. Possibly the so-called *presentatives* are like that, for example, the "voici" and "voilà" of French or the "vot" and "von" of Russian. In English, as far as I can tell, the only word which is obligatorily accompanied by a gesture is the nonstandard size-demonstrating word "yea" as in "She's about yea tall."

Place indications take part in the deictic system of a language by virtue of the fact that for many locating expressions, the location of one, or another, or both, of the speech act participants can serve as a spatial reference point. Sometimes all that means is that for an expression which in a nondeictic use requires mention of a reference object, in its deictic use the reference object, taken to be the speaker's body at the time of the speech act, simply goes unmentioned.

Take, for example, the expression "upstairs". If I say, "Johnny lives upstairs," you will understand me as meaning upstairs of the place where I am at the time I say the sentence, unless the immediately preceding discourse has provided some other reference point. If I say "Harry lives nearby," the same can be said. You will understand that Harry lives near to the place where I am when I say the sentence, again, except for the case where a reference point has been identified in the immediately preceding discourse.

For words that can refer to areas or spaces, the word "this" followed by the appropriate noun locates an object as being in the same area as the speaker is at coding time. Thus I can talk about something being "in this room", "on this planet", "in this city", etc. In the Fijian language, I am told, the choice of different prepositions has that same function. If I want to say, in Fijian, that somebody is in a certain town, I will choose one word for "in" if I am in that same town, another if I am not.

The English adverb "here", when used for locating objects, is paraphrasable as "in this place", "at this place", etc., in either the gestural or the symbolic use of "this". The scope of the word "here" is as general, or as vague, as the scope of the noun "place". With the scope usually determinable from the subject matter, I can use the word "here" to mean anything from "at this point" to "in this galaxy".

Systems of place-deictic adverbs and demonstratives seem to be of various types, according to the number of distinct terms that can be used. In English we have a two-way contrast shown in the pair "this" versus "that", though we also have the archaic forms "yon" and "yonder". In a number of languages, the system of contrasts involves three terms, as with the Japanese "kore", "sore", and "are". One is told that Tlingit is a language with a four-way contrast, translatable, I suppose, as "right here", "right there", "over there", and "way the heck over there".

The various terms in these systems may differ according to whether they can be used gesturally, symbolically, or anaphorically. There may be differences, in fact, between the adverbs and the demonstratives in this regard, even though both might have the same number of terms. And there can be differences from one dialect to another. For example, in standard Japanese, the two distal locative adverbs, namely "soko" and "asoko", differ in that while both can be used gesturally, only "soko" can be used anaphorically. There appear to be dialect differences with respect to this observation, analogously, I suppose, to the differences in Scots dialects between those in which the word "yonder" can be used only when the object being located is presently visible, and those which do not require this.

It is frequently the case that if a language has two or more terms in its system of place-deictic categories, one of these will identify the location of the speaker, or the speaker and addressee as a group, and one can indicate the location of the addressee whenever the addressee's location is taken as being distinct from that of the speaker. This latter appears to be one of the functions of the middle category for such languages as Japanese, Spanish, or Tagalog, but the words seem to have so many other functions, as well, that it is difficult to be absolutely clear about the reference to the conversation partners.

I have heard of one language, Samal, with place-deictic terms which separately indicate the position of the speaker, the addressee, the audience, and "none of the above". In this language, spoken in the Philippines and studied by Bill Geoghegan, there are separate place deictic expressions for "near me", "near you", "near other participants in our conversation" and "away from all of the above". The way Geoghegan explained it to me, if A is talking to B and C is a part of their conversational group, A will use one deictic category for locating things which are near C; if C is not a part of the conversational group, as might be the case if he has fallen asleep or if A and B are whispering or if C has picked up a newspaper or has started talking to somebody else, then A must use the fourth place-deictic category instead of the third.

When I talked about non-deictic place indications, I discussed the various terms that depend on the understanding of something being oriented in space in a particular way, and it was in this connection that I examined expressions like "in front of", "behind", "above", "below", "to the left side of", and "to the right side of". The way we understood these expressions, especially those connected with the horizontal dimensions, depended on how we imputed an orientation in space to the reference object. These expressions have additionally a use that shows up in deictically anchored situations. In particular, the location of the speaker and his outlook on the world can determine the orientation of the objects around him. From the fact that we can speak of "the side of the tree *facing* me", we see that even things which do not have front/back orientation of their own can be thought of as having their *front* close to the observer. If there is a kitten on the ground close to a tree, and close to the side which "faces" me, I can say that there is a kitten "in front of" the tree.

If there is a dog on the opposite side of the tree I can say that it is "behind" the tree. Notice that these expressions cannot be interpreted apart from knowing where I am at the time I utter the sentences. In this egocentric way of recognizing orientation in space, "left" and "right" are defined from the observer's point of view.

Thus, if the dog and the cat should walk ninety degrees widdershins around the tree, I can then speak of the dog as being on the left side of the tree and the kitten on the right side of the tree.

The conditions that I have mentioned so far are satisfactory for thinking aloud, but for deictic locating expressions involving notions like "front", "back", "left", and "right", the speaker must also be aware of his addressee's point of view. He can use these abbreviated expressions only when speaker and hearer are oriented toward the object in the same way. Thus, if I ask you "What's the shiny object out there to the left of the cypress tree?" I've spoken appropriately only if you and I are both oriented toward these objects in the same way; it is inappropriate if the tree is between us and I am talking to you over the telephone. In situations in which I recognize that your point of view may be different from mine, I must use expressions which show that fact, such expressions as "to your right", or "on the right side as you face it".

I have spoken here about spatial orientation concepts which are defined from the speaker's point of view. It should be clear that it is also possible for the speaker of a sentence to regard his own body as a physical object with an orientation in space; expressions like "in front of me", "behind me", or "on my left side", are deictic by containing a first person pronoun but they are not instances of the deictic use of the orientational expressions.

Place deixis plays a role in description of movement verbs in ways that I suggested in the first lecture, and there is much to say about that particular class of verbs. In fact, I plan to take up problems connected with coming and going, coming and going home, and coming and going away, in a later lecture. There are many ways of using place-deictic terms that reflect what might be called *taking the other fellow's point of view*. I'll discuss these matters when I talk about social deixis. There are special uses of place-deictic terms in third-person narratives. I'll take that up in a lecture on discourse.

The category needed for time deixis, as I mentioned earlier, is what we might call *coding time*. By coding time I mean, in general, the time of the "communication act", but of course there is some unclarity in that expression. In particular, there is a need to distinguish encoding time from decoding time, to talk about a number of problems connected with messages that are not sent and received at the same time; and there is the problem of knowing whether the coding time is understood broadly as the time during which the utterance as a whole is being produced, or the precise time at which the deictic time word is being uttered. Just as the same gestural element can occur in accompaniment with two or more different gestures in a single sentence, as with "I want you to put *this* block on top of *this* one," the word "now" can be used in two voice gestural ways in a single utterance, as, for example, "Now you see it, now you don't."

In general anyway, the main purpose of the proximal deictic time category is that of identifying a particular time as coinciding with, being close to, or being contained in the same larger time unit as, the moment of speech, or the coding time. The terms past, present, and future refer to times earlier than, coinciding with, or later than, the time of the speech act. Here too, the notion "time of the speech act" has an undesired vagueness. One can imagine a skillful dentist extracting a loose tooth saying something like "This won't take long, did it?" For the interpretation of that sentence we would have to assume that whatever took place happened after the dentist started talking and before he finished talking.

We can talk about something occurring simultaneously with the speech act, or as having an extent which includes the moment of the speech act, as in "I want you to turn the corner ... right ... now" for the first case, or "John lives in Chicago now," for the second case.

There is a general vagueness associated with "now" like what we found for "here", but again the word "right" can narrow things down a bit. As we could say "right here", we could also say "right now". Again, in the expression with "right", the addressee is assumed to be monitoring the message as it is being produced, and is therefore able to identify the intended time point. There is another narrowing word, "just", as in "just now", but it is generally used to indicate a short period of time *before* the coding time. In Russian the word "sejchas" can be used to refer to a time period either immediately before or immediately after the coding time, and therefore it has the function of both "just now" and "right away". American tourists in Russia are sometimes confused by the fact that so many guides translate the Russian "sejchas" consistently into "just now", and use it to refer to times which immediately follow the speech act time as well as those which immediately precede. "We'll visit the mausoleum just now."

Time periods that are located at measured or unmeasured distances earlier than or later than the coding time call for adverbs like "recently" or "soon", or measurement expressions like "three days ago" or "ten years from now". For something which continues from the moment of speech into the future, the word "henceforth" is appropriate; for something which is going to occur at a particular time in the future, an expression like "later on" is appropriate. The full story will reveal a large number of interesting differences between time-indicating expressions depending on whether they are used deictically. Some occur only in deictic expressions. "After a while" can be used either deictically or non-deictically, but "in a while" is used only deictically, and "after a while" is at least most natural when used deictically. I can say "I'll do that in a while," but not "I did it in a while." Expressions of later time having the form "in" plus "a" plus the name of a noncalendric time unit are used in nondeictic contexts only with completive aspect verbs, but in a deictic context they can indicate a period before the end of which the thing will happen. Thus, if I say "I did it in an hour" the meaning is that it took me an hour to do it, and that I finished doing it; if I say "I'll do it in an hour" it can have that use, but it can also mean that I'll do it before an hour runs out, even if I don't start doing it until 45 minutes from now.

We noticed in the discussion of place deixis that there were ways of locating something within the same area as the speaker, as in an expression like "in this town", or "in this room". Similarly, there are expressions indicating the time of an event as occurring within the same time unit as the moment of the speech act, and, once again, the demonstrative "this" is called for. I must remind you here of the difference between calendric and noncalendric time units, and the difference between positional and nonpositional calendric units. If I wish to locate the time of an event within the same calendric nonpositional unit as the moment of speech, I use the word "this" with the name of that unit, with certain special qualifications regarding the day-length units. If something happened or is to happen "this week", its occurrence is in the same week as the coding time of the utterance; for something which happens "this month", "this year", or "this century", again the pattern is the same: its occurrence is placed within the same calendric unit as the moment of speech.

For the positional calendric units, matters are slightly different. If I say that something happened or is to happen "this August", I am saying that it will occur within the August period of the calendar year which contains the coding time. If I speak of something occurring on "this Thursday", I speak of it as occurring on a Thursday of the calendar week which also contains the coding time. For the months of the year, the interpretation is fairly straightforward, because the full sequence of month names is included within a calendar year, so that there is no confusion about the identity of the first month and the last month. With the days of the week, however, things are a bit tricky, for two reasons. One is the uncertainty over whether the week begins with Sunday or Monday, the other is the dialect difference between speakers of English who do or do not use "this" plus a weekday name only for identifying times which are within the same calendar week but are later than the coding time. With the names of the seasons and with the subdivisions of the twenty-four hour day, however, it is not always clear what the larger including unit is. If I say "this afternoon", everybody knows that I am talking about the afternoon of the day which includes the coding time, and if I say "this summer", everybody knows that I am talking about something taking place during the summer of the calendar year which includes the coding time, but since there is a year change during the winter and a day change during the night, expressions like "this winter" and "this night" (except when resolved by the tense of the accompanying verb) are potentially ambiguous when spoken during any other time of the year or the day.

There are also ways of locating an event with respect to the coding time as occurring in a calendric unit which is at such and such a distance from the calendric unit that includes the coding time. In English the word "next" indicates the unit which follows the current unit, "last" indicates the unit which precedes the current unit, the locutions "after next" and "before last" being usable for the calendric units that are two units away, in the past and in the future, from the current one. Thus we have "this week", "next week", "week after next", or "last week", "week before last". This pattern holds for weeks, months, years, as well, I suppose, as less commonly used units such as decades and centuries.

Some of the deictic calendric units are given separate lexicalizations, and these may be different from language to language.

In English, for example, instead of "this day" we have "today"; instead of "next day" we have "tomorrow" and so on. For the day subdivisions we have "this afternoon", "this morning", "this evening", but a separate lexicalization for "this night", namely "tonight". (The "night" that is lexicalized in "tonight" is the "night" period that is seen as being a part of the calendar day. In this way "tonight" differs from the expressions "last night" or "night before last".) Many languages have a richer set of lexicalizations for the deictic day names than English does, having, for example, separate words for yesterday, day before yesterday, the day before the day before yesterday, etc. The Persian system goes two days ahead and four days back; Japanese goes three days ahead and three days back and so does Russian; Vietnamese goes three days ahead and four days back; Chinantec goes four days ahead and four days back. The deictic day subdivisions might be separately lexicalized. In many languages, the word for "this morning" or "this evening" is a separate lexical item.

In Chinantec, there is a separate lexical item for yesterday afternoon, and another separate lexical item for the afternoon of the day before yesterday.

Sometimes you will find a separate way of indicating a positional deictic unit depending on whether that unit contains the moment of speech or not. In English, we can say "this morning" during the morning or later on during the day. In Chinantec, on the other hand, there is one way of saying "this morning" during the morning, another way of saying it during the rest of the day.

English has something analogous to that with the names of the days of the week. There are two uses of expressions having the form "this" plus a weekday name. One is that of identifying the day as a whole, and in this usage there are no restrictions on which day of the week it can be used. Thus, if I am talking about the current Wednesday and I am speaking on that Wednesday, I can say something like "This Wednesday the weather is a lot better than last Wednesday"; but, assuming that I know today is Wednesday, I would not say "I am planning to have dinner in Santa Cruz this Wednesday". The reason seems to be that the deictic day words, namely, "today", "tomorrow", "yesterday", seem to have priority over these other expressions when you are locating the time of some event. Thus, for example, if I know it is Wednesday when I am talking, and I wish to speak of something that is to happen on the following day, it is not appropriate for me to say that it is going to happen "this Thursday", but I must say that it is going to happen "tomorrow".

I mentioned that there is one set of conventions followed by many speakers of English by which the dating expressions of the form "this" followed by a weekday name are used only of times which follow, within the same week, the coding time. For speakers of this dialect, because of the priority of the deictic day names, there is never any need for the expression "this Monday", and none of these expressions can be used on a Saturday. This is true no matter where your week begins, because if your week ends on Saturday, there are no following days within the same week, and if your week ends on Sunday, the only day which follows Saturday is its immediate successor, and that calls for the word "tomorrow" rather than "this Sunday".

Expressions like "this Friday" or "this April" identify, in dating expressions, a positional unit within the same larger calendar unit as the coding time. Without the use of the demonstratives, expressions like "in April" or "on Friday" can be used in dating something within the named positional unit which is at a distance from the coding time or less than one noncalendric larger unit, in either the future or the past depending on the tense of the clause. Thus, if on Monday I say "I saw her on Friday", I am talking about the immediately preceding Friday; if I say "I'll see her on Friday," I am talking about the immediately following Friday.

The use of the words "next" and "last" with the positional calendric terms has speakers of English divided into an uncountable number of subdialects, and I believe the best thing to do is to leave this subject untouched.

The tense systems of a number of languages do more than simply indicate the "direction" in earlier or later time of the event but sometimes make some reference to a calendric unit. Thus, as I learned from SIL. linguist Robert Russell, the Amahauca language of Peru has one tense form which identifies a period since the last full moon, and it has another tense form which means "yesterday" if it is pronounced during the morning but means "this morning" if it is pronounced later on in the day.

Digression: While I am on the subject of the ways in which the use of a linguistic expression requires the speaker's awareness of the time of day, I should point out that the traditional greetings in a great many languages are selected according to the time of day, as, for example, English "good morning" and "good afternoon" and the like. The one example of a naming expression whose appropriateness is determined by the time of day in which it is used is an example I have from Charles Ferguson and which I have managed to bring into every lecture I've ever given on the subject of deixis. In Moroccan Arabic there are two words for needle; one of them is used only in the morning, and the other is used during the rest of the day.

In my discussion of time, I referred many times to the property of its being unidirectional. It happens that with a number of deictic expressions of time, this unidirectionality is ignored. In a great many languages, for example, the word for "yesterday" is the same as the word for "tomorrow", the word for "the day before yesterday" being the same as the word for "the day after tomorrow" and so on. Hindi is one such language. It is typical of the Shiriana languages of South America that their tenses are determined independently of the difference between past and future. The tense system in these languages distinguishes such notions as a period a few minutes from the moment of speech, a period within the same calendar day as the moment of speech, a period within a few days of the moment of speech, a period significantly more remote than that, etc., but all independently of past and future.

I mentioned earlier that many locutions about time involve spatial metaphors based on the notion of movement. It is on the moving world version of the metaphor that we can speak of the future as being ahead and the past as being behind; it is the moving time version of the metaphor which gives Vietnamese its time expressions, "the week ahead" for "last week" and "the week behind" for "next week", and so on. In English, too, we speak of "this coming Tuesday", suggesting the image that Tuesday is moving towards us, not that we are moving towards it.

An expression like "Summer has come and gone" is based on the same image.

I will say more about coming and going in the next lecture, and I will say more about tense in the final lecture. Situations for which encoding time and decoding time need to be distinguished will be mentioned in my discussion of social deixis, under the general heading of taking the other fellow's point of view. At the end of my second lecture on deixis I will summarize the uses of demonstratives in English.

Twenty-five years later: There are now lots of things to read on the topics taken up in this chapter. Erving Goffman (1979)[1] makes a number of distinctions about the ways in which one can participate in a speaking event. Clifford Hill has done numerous studies on both language-dependent and situation-dependent ways of treating non-oriented reference objects in locating expressions (Hill 1975, 1978).[2] J. Peter Denny has described the elaborate demonstrative system of the Inuktitut lan-

---

1. Erving Goffman, Footing, *Semiotica* 25:1–29 (1979).
2. Clifford A. Hill, Variation in the Use of Front and Back by Bilingual Speakers, in *Pro-*

guage (Denny 1980).[3] I have treated some issues in the description of demonstrative categories in Fillmore (1982).[4] Geoffrey Nunberg has clarified many of the problems associated with the "anchoring" of certain implicit-anchor temporal or spatial terms such as "local", "recent", etc., in Nunberg (1993).[5] There are several collections of studies of deictic systems and deictic practices, e.g., Jarvella and Klein (1982),[6] Rauh (1983),[7] and Morel and Danon-Boileau (1992).[8]

ceedings of the Fourth Annual Meeting of the Berkeley Linguistics Society (Berkeley, CA: Berkeley Linguistics Society, 1975), and

Clifford A. Hill, Linguistic Representation of Spatial and Temporal Orientation, in Proceedings of the Fourth Annual Meeting of the Berkeley Linguistics Society (Berkeley, CA: Berkeley Linguistics Society, 1978).

3. J. Peter Denny, Semantics of the Inuktitut (Eskimo) spatial deictics, Research Bulletin No. 352 (Department of Psychology, Western Ontario University, 1980).

4. Charles J. Fillmore, Towards a descriptive framework for spatial deixis, in Speech, Place and Action: Studies in deixis and related topics, ed. Robert J. Jarvella and Wolfgang Klein (Chichester: Wiley, 1982).

5. Geoffrey Nunberg, Indexicality and Deixis, Linguistics and Philosophy 7:243–286 (1993).

6. Robert J. Jarvella and Wolfgang Klein, eds., Speech, Place and Action: Studies in Deixis and Related Topics (Chichester: Wiley, 1982).

7. Gisa Rauh, ed., Essays on Deixis (Tübingen: Gunter Narr, 1983).

8. Mary-Annick Morel and Laurent Danon-Boileau, eds., La Deixis (Colloque en Sorbonne: Presses Universitaires de France, 1992).

COMING AND GOING[1]

In two papers of mine, published in 1965 and 1966,[2] I presented an analysis of the appropriateness conditions for deictically anchored English sentences containing the motion verbs "come" and "go". The main conclusion I arrived at in those papers was that, while the directional complement of the verb "go" signals movement to a place where the speaker (or encoder) is not located at coding time, the destination associated with expressions containing the verb "come" requires somewhat more complicated understandings. The place to which one speaks of something or somebody "coming" is understood as a place where either the speaker or the addressee is located at either the coding time or the reference time. In Fillmore (1969),[3] I reviewed these findings and added a remark on the function of the verb "come" in sentences which are not deictically anchored with respect to speaker and addressee. In third-person narrative, my point was, the choice of the verb "come" was determined by whether the narrator regards the destination of the movement as being the location at reference-time of the *central character* of the episode to which the sentence has reference. Then in 1970,[4] I repeated that claim and added something that I took as distributional evidence for it, namely, the observation that—certain conditions being satisfied—a single sentence cannot combine references to separate journeys with differing destinations by using the verb "come" for each journey. My evidence was that while the first of the following two sentences is acceptable, the second is not:

1. An abridgment of this lecture appeared, under the title "How to Know Whether You're Coming or Going," in *Linguistik 1971*, ed. K. Hyldgaard-Jensen (Athenäeum, 1972) pp. 269–279.
2. Charles J. Fillmore, Entailment Rules in a Semantic Theory, in *The Ohio State University Project on Linguistic Analysis*, Report No. 11 (1965), and Deictic Categories in the Semantics of 'Come', in *Foundations of Language*, Vol. 2 (1966) pp. 219–227.
3. Charles J. Fillmore, Types of Lexical Information, in *Studies in Syntax and Semantics*, ed. Ferenc Kiefer (Dordrecht: Reidel, 1969) pp. 109–137.
4. Charles J. Fillmore, Subjects, Speakers and Roles, *Synthèse*, Vol. 21 (1970) pp. 251–274.

After John came to Bill's house, John and Bill together went over to Mary's house.

After John came to Bill's house, John and Bill together came over to Mary's house.

Then in 1971, a few weeks ago, I carried out a particularly significant piece of research into the meaning of these very interesting verbs: I looked them up in the dictionary.

'The dictionary' in this case, was the Oxford English Dictionary (O.E.D.). The 'signification' part of the entry for "come" in the O.E.D. looks like this:

> An elementary intransitive verb of motion expressing movement towards or so as to reach the speaker, or the person spoken to, or towards a point where the speaker in thought or imagination places himself, or (when he himself is not in question) towards the person who forms the subject of his narrative.

Motion toward the speaker or the person spoken to is, of course, motion toward the encoder's or decoder's location at coding time. Motion toward a point where the speaker in thought or imagination places himself can be thought of as motion toward the assumed location of a participant in the conversation at reference time. The case where the speaker himself is not in question is the case of a third-person or non-person-deictically anchored discourse, and the person who forms the subject of the narrative is the central character that I had discussed.

In the relevant part of the definition of "go" where "go" is seen as paired with "come", the O.E.D. has this to say:

> (Where) the prominent notion is that of destination or direction … the verb is distinguished from COME by the implication that the movement is not towards the speaker, or the person whose point of view he for the moment assumes.

Finding out that something has been known, in its basic outlines, for a very long time, in no way detracts from the inherent interest that the facts may have, so I think it will be very much worth our while to look into the semantics of the *deictic motion verbs* today, between the first and second of my two lectures on deixis proper. We will, in fact, come up with a few things that are not derivable from the O.E.D. account.

I will first of all say something about a number of general concepts associated with locomotion; I will then characterize the English deictic motion verbs–"come", "go", "bring", and "take"–with a remark or two on their kin in other languages; lastly I will discuss the transferred uses of "come" in third-person narrative. I mentioned in my earlier lectures the use of "come" and "go" in expressions relating to the passing of time. I won't say more about that today.

First, on motion. We say of something that it has moved, in the "locomotion" sense of movement that I have in mind, if it is at one location at one time and at another location at another time. I will disregard such self-contained instances of motion as wiggling and rotating, and I will also disregard unbounded instances of locomotion of the sort planets enjoy. I will discuss *bounded motion*, motion that can be characterized as having a starting point and an ending point, an origin and a destination, a Source and a Goal. In addition to the terminals, we can also characterize or delimit in some way the intervening states which we might call, after David Bennett,[5] the Path. (Whenever we want our discourse about these matters to sound more serious, we may substitute for the terms Source, Goal, and Path, the terms Ablative, Allative and Itinerative.)

Motion, thus, presupposes an understanding of both time and space. We can characterize the initial state as the doublet P_1T_1, with P and T standing for Place and Time respectively, and we can identify the final state of the motion as the doublet P_nT_n. The set of states P_iT_i (with "i" between 1 and n) identifies the Path.

---

5. David C. Bennett, *Spatial and Temporal Uses of English Prepositions: An Essay in Stratificational Semantics* (London: Longman, 1975).

Recall now that I introduced the notion *reference time* in an earlier lecture, meaning by that the point or period that is the temporal focus or background for the event or condition being described in the clause. The reference time can be made explicit by means of a *time specifier* phrase. The reference time for a clause indicating motion can either be a span which covers the whole period T_1–T_n or it can be identified with either T_1 or T_n. (It's not quite this simple, but what I'm telling you isn't all wrong, either.) Examples of sentences in which the reference time is the time of the whole journey are these:

She swam from the end of the dock to the shore.

He travelled from Columbus to Biloxi.

If we were to add time phrases like "this morning" or "last week" we would be locating the whole journey in time.

But now consider the verbs "leave" and "arrive" in expressions in which only the Goal phrase is explicitly present. I would like to say of the sentences

He left for Chicago around noon.

and

He arrived in Chicago around noon.

that the reference time is T_1 for the first sentence and T_n for the second. This may all seem too obvious to deserve mention, but we will find it necessary to distinguish between *departure time* (T_1) and *arrival time* (T_n) when we talk about the deictic motion verbs, as I think you will agree if you think about these sentences

He went home around midnight.

He came home around midnight.

The time specifier in the first sentence could be understood as indicating the time he left the party, say; the one in the second sentence indicates the time he arrived home.

80

In the first of those sentences we feel intuitively that there is in the setting or in the previous discourse a location that is a kind of spatial reference point for the sentence, namely the place where, say, a party was going on. What I'm saying is that for a sentence like "He went home around midnight" there is in the discourse not only a presupposed time period onto which the interpreter can anchor the sentence, but also a presupposed location—in this case, the place *from* which the movement began.

Since there are so many parallels between space and time expressions, I may as well tell you about another one that I think I see. Not only can we speak of reference time, it is also useful to speak of *reference place*, the location or object that is taken as the framework or spatial reference point for what is mentioned in the clause. On the one hand the reference place can be either the location of an event that does not involve locomotion or the location of all of the points in an instance of locomotion, and on the other hand it can be either the place which is identified with the Source of the motion, or the place which is identified with the Goal of the motion. The choice is frequently determined by the semantics of the verb. Certain verbs have reference places identified with P_1, the Source (for example, "leave", and "go" in one of its uses), others have reference places identified with P_n, the Goal (for example, "arrive" and "come"), and still others have reference places that are not uniquely identified with either of these (for example, "travel", and "go" in another of its uses). In a sentence like

People kept coming and going all day.

the same reference place is understood as the arrival point or P_n for the "coming" and the departure point or P_1 for the "going".

This place/time parallelism exists on the deictic level as well, and the whole thing becomes fairly easy to conceptualize if we can think of a communication act as metaphorically an instance of motion—the travelling of a message from one person to another. Whenever the time period or time span determining the center of the tense system is simply taken to be the time during which the communication act as a whole takes place, we may simply speak of *coding time*. (This, of course, is the typical situation for speech, since spoken messages are usually received at the same time they are sent.)

If the center for the tense system is the time the message is being encoded, we speak of *encoding time*, as exemplified in a written message like

I'm writing this letter on the balcony of my hotel in Debrecen.

where the tense center is taken to be the time the message is being interpreted, we can speak of *decoding time*, as exemplified in

You have just read my last letter to you.

Viewing communication as analogous to motion, we can see that the encoding time is T_1, the decoding time is T_n, and the coding time in general is the time span T_1–T_n. Similarly, when sender and receiver are both "in the same place", we can speak of the *coding place*, as in

It sure is nice here now, isn't it?

where the encoder's and decoder's locations are distinct, we can speak of the *encoding place*, the encoder's location, and the *decoding place*, the decoder's location. Both are indicated in the next sentence.

It's nice over here, what's it like over there?

Now to the *deictic motion verbs*. What is there to say about the verbs "come" and "go" in English, and about the verbs "bring" and "take"? Description of these verbs will obviously need to mention something about the location of the conversation participants, and what we need to do now is to make sure we can be clear about the details. My method will be that of proposing, disconfirming, and revising hypotheses. I will begin by considering only uses of the verbs in person-deictically-anchored discourse, that is, in discourse in which the speaker and the addressee figure as relevant landmarks.

Sometimes we find, in descriptions of exotic languages, grammatical categories associated with, say, directional affixes of some sort, that are named "Toward Speaker" and "Away from Speaker". Let's take it as our first hypothesis that "come" and "bring" have to do with motion toward the speaker, "go" and "take" with motion away from the speaker.

> Hypothesis I: (a) "come" and "bring" indicate motion toward the location of the speaker at coding time; (b) "go" and "take" indicate motion toward a location which is distinct from the speaker's location at coding time.

> Fancy Version of Hypothesis I: (a) for the movements indicated with "come" and "bring", the encoder is at P_n at T_n; (b) for the movements indicated with "go" and "take", the encoder is at P_1 at T_1.

Nondisconfirming observations are easy to find, as, for example, sentences like the following:

> Please come in.

> Please go away.

Disconfirming sentences are also easy to find, unfortunately for Hypothesis I, as, for example, the sentences

> He had come here two hours before I arrived.

> I just saw him go from over there to way over there.

The first of these refers to motion toward a place where the speaker is at coding time, and "there" is, at the very least, a place where the speaker is not present at the coding time. A hypothesis compatible with all of the above examples is that the verbs have to do with "motion toward here" as opposed to "motion toward there", the two deictic adverbs understood as having their symbolic and not their gestural (or anaphoric) senses.

> Hypothesis II: (a) "come" and "bring" indicate motion toward the location of the speaker at coding time; (b) "go" and "take"

indicate motion toward a location which is distinct from the speaker's location at coding time.

Fancy Version of Hypothesis II: (a) for the movements indicated with "come" and "bring", the encoder is at Pn at coding time; (b) for the movements indicated with "go" and "take", the encoder is not at Pn at coding time.

Ungrammatical sentences whose nongrammaticality is accounted for by Hypothesis II include such as

*Please go here.

*They went here.

*Take them here.

(I restricted the way we were to understand the adverb "here" as *symbolic* rather than *gestural*. In the gestural use, as in pointing to locations on a map, these sentences are perfectly acceptable.)

But now let's consider some more sentences. The first two do not disconfirm the hypothesis.

I'll take it there right away.

I'll go there right away.

But the next two that I'll give you raise some questions about the (a) part of the hypothesis, the part relating to "come" and "bring".

I'll bring it there right away.

I'll come there right away.

The destination of the movements in these cases is neither the encoder's location at arrival time, nor his location at coding time. It's not the first, because, since I chose first-person subject examples, it is the encoder whose movements are in question; it's not the second, because of the way we understand the adverb "there" symbolically.

In the case of these last sentences, the destination is understood as the place where the decoder is at coding time. If I say that I'll come there right away, what I have to be talking about is the place where *you* are now. In these sentences, the encoder was the mover, but even if we had taken a third-person subject, as in

He'll come there right away.

we would still have the same understanding about the decoder's being "there" at coding time.

This leads us to reformulate the hypothesis, so that the part relating to "come" will identify the destination of the movement as a place where either the encoder or the decoder is at coding time.

Hypothesis III: "come" and "bring" indicate motion toward the location of either the speaker or the addressee at coding time.

Fancy Version of Hypothesis III: for the movements indicated with "come" or "bring", Pn is the location at coding time of either the encoder or the decoder.

Thus we see that the criteria by which a location can be the destination for "come" or "bring" as opposed to "go" or "take", are different from those for selecting the place-indicator "here" as opposed to "there". "Here" cannot refer to the decoding place, if that is distinct from the encoding place.

The pronoun "we" can be understood inclusively or exclusively, as we saw earlier. In a sentence like

Can we go over there?

the pronoun is ambiguous between these two readings; but in a sentence like

Can we come over there?

the pronoun can be understood exclusively only. The destination for "come" has to include either the speaker or the addressee, but since the pronoun "we" has to include the speaker, we must conclude that the destination for that sentence is the place where the addressee is at coding time. The ambiguity of the first sentence, the unambiguous character of the second sentence, are accounted for by Hypothesis III.

In certain constructions, we know that the first-person-plural pronoun is *only* understood inclusively, as, for example, in the so-called first-person-plural imperative construction with "let's". In a sentence like

Let's go over there.

all is well, since you and I can both go to a place where I am not now; but a sentence like

*Let's come over there.

is bad, because you and I cannot both go to a place where one of us already is. Again, Hypothesis III provides the principles by which these facts on ambiguity and grammaticality can be explained.

But Hypothesis III can't stand after all. There are situations in which we can talk about somebody betaking himself to a place where neither speaker nor addressee is at coding time, and yet where the verb "come" is quite appropriate. Consider the case where you and I are together in the same room and I say to you,

I'll come there at dawn.

In this sentence, "there" is neither the encoding place nor the decoding place. It's not the encoding place by definition, and it's not the decoding place by hypothesis, since I asked you to imagine that you and I were together. I think it's clear that what I would have to mean by "there" in that sentence is a place where you will be at the reference time (which, with this verb, is the arrival time). On the other hand, in a sentence like

Please come there at dawn.

when said under the same conditions, "there" cannot refer to the decoder's location at arrival time, since it is the decoder whose motion is in question. For this last sentence, "there" is understood as the encoder's location at reference time.

We are ready for another formulation of our account of "come" and "bring".

> Hypothesis IV: "come" and "bring" indicate motion toward the location of either the speaker or the addressee at either coding time or reference time.

> Fancy Version of Hypothesis IV: for the movements indicated with "come" or "bring" Pn is the location at Tn or at coding time of either the encoder or the decoder.

In the examples which led up to this formulation, the mover was one of the conversation participants, the destination was the location at the time of reference of the other participant. I'm going to where you will be, or you're going to be where I will be. If the subject of the verb is somebody other than either of the conversation partners, as in

> He'll come there at dawn.

the sentence is ambiguous, permitting either the understanding that you will be there when he arrives, or that I will be. In a sentence like

> We'll come there at dawn.

as compared with

> We'll go there at dawn.

the pronoun is unambiguously exclusive of addressee, since the sentence has to be understood as motion toward the addressee's location. Again, while a sentence like

> Let's go there at dawn.

is all right, we will find it unacceptable to say

> *Let's come there at dawn.

I've been using the word "there" in most of these examples merely to limit ourselves to the situation in which the destination is a place where the encoder cannot be at coding time; and by placing both participants in the same location, I was able to remove temporarily from consideration the possibility that the destination was the place where the decoder was at coding time. Now if we take a sentence which has no other place-deictic or person-deictic elements apart from the verb "come" and ask ourselves under what conditions it could appropriately be used, we will come up with the conclusions that I presented in my first lecture. Thus, the conditions under which I can say to you,

Johnny came to the office yesterday morning.

include the cases where I am at the office when I say it, you are at the office when I say it, I was in the office yesterday morning when Johnny came, or you were there then.

To repeat myself, the destination for "come", unless certain cases are ruled out by the presence of other deictic information, is either the encoder's or the decoder's location at either coding time or reference time. The destination for "go", on the other hand, is quite simply a place which is distinct from the encoder's location at coding time. It follows from this difference that there are many situations where either "go" or "come" would be appropriate. It's okay to say either

He'll go to the office tomorrow to pick me up.

He'll come to the office tomorrow to pick me up.

even when the encoder is not in the office at coding time; and, with similar conditions, the next two sentences are also equally okay.

She'll go there to meet you.

She'll come there to meet you.

For these last examples I've concentrated on "come" and "go" and ignored "bring" and "take". In general, "bring" and "take" have the same possibilities as "come" and "go", with respect to their destinations, but "bring", at least in many dialects, is subject to fewer conditions than

"come". I suspect that in some dialects "bring" has no deictic compo-
nents at all, but is merely a destination-oriented verb having much the
same syntactic nature as "deliver". Everybody agrees that

*Let's come there.

is bad, but many people allow themselves to say things like

Let's bring it there.

I'm guessing now when I say that: in some dialects, the appropriateness conditions for "bring" are essentially the same as those for "come";
in some the word is like "deliver"; and in the majority dialect there is a
requirement that the destination be a place where a *person* having some
importance in the discourse is located. My evidence for this claim is
that many people who would allow themselves to say "Let's bring it
there" when talking about delivering a box of candy to a friend in a
hospital, would not say it when talking about transporting a flag, say, to
the top of a hill on an uninhabited island.

The verbs "bring" and "take", by the way, have different senses that
are relevant to our discussion, and we will shortly discover a need to
keep them apart. A sentence of the form "A brings B to C" is paraphrasable as either "A enables B to come to C" or "A comes to C with B accompanying him", or "A comes to C conveying B". We may call these the
enabling, the *conducting*, and the *conveying* senses of "bring", and we
will notice that "take" has likewise three such senses, constructed out of
the paraphrases I suggested for "bring" by substituting "go" for "come".

The enabling sense shows up in sentences like:

A grant from the Ford Foundation brought me to California.

Fifty bucks will take me to Fresno.

The conducting sense is found in sentences like:

She brought me to this party.

Please take me away.

The conveying sense is seen in sentences like:

I brought it in my pocket.

I took it to the laundry.

In some languages we find the conducting and conveying meanings separately lexicalized, but not lexicalized with the *deictic motion verbs*. I have in mind expressions like Japanese "turete kuru/iku" ("come/go accompanying") and "motte kuru/iku" ("come/go carrying").

Even apart from special problems connected with "bring", Hypothesis IV turns out to be unsatisfactory. Consider now sentences like these:

He came over to my place last night, but I wasn't home.

I came over to your place last night, but you weren't home.

opposed to one like:

*I came over to Fred's place last night, but he wasn't home.

which is unacceptable.

In the acceptable cases, the destination of "come" is not a place where either participant is at coding time or was at reference time, but is understood as the *home base* of one of them. The home base need not be the home base at coding time, because we find acceptable sentences like this one:

When you lived on Sixth Street, I came over several times to visit you, but nobody was ever home.

John Lawler pointed out to me that the home base must be the person's home base at reference time, since it is not acceptable, in the home base interpretation, to say

I came over to that house about a week before you bought it.

Here is the latest version of our hypothesis for "come" and "bring", modified to include the home base notion.

Hypothesis V: "come" and "bring" indicate motion toward the

location of either the speaker or the addressee at either coding time or reference time, or toward the location of the home base of either the speaker or the hearer at reference time.

Fancy Version of Hypothesis V: for the movements indicated with "come" or "bring", Pn is either the location at Tn of the encoder, the encoder's home, the decoder, or the decoder's home, or it is the location of the encoder or the decoder at coding time.

But now let's look at some problems connected with sentences which make explicit reference to somebody's home–sentences containing the adverb "home". The word can be used to indicate Location, Source, Path, or Goal, as in sentences such as:

Is Johnny home?

Fred left home this morning.

Sheila left for home an hour ago.

George arrived home after midnight.

(I assume that in the "leave for home" case, although the word "home" identifies the Goal, the phrase "for home" seems rather to indicate the Path.) The word "home" is to be understood as meaning "x's home", and the question I'd like us to consider now is that of identifying "x".)

In the locative expressions, "home" designates the home of the person about whose location something is being said. In the motion sentences, it would appear that the home is the home of the person indicated by the subject of the motion verb. Let's represent this as Hypothesis A.

Hypothesis A: the construction *motion verb* + "*home*" indicates motion toward the home of the person designated by the subject phrase of the motion verb.

There are many sentences which support this hypothesis. In

Johnny went home.

we understand it that where Johnny went was his own home. In

Johnny came home.

we have that understanding again, but this time with the additional understandings predictable from Hypothesis V. In

I'm going to go home now.

we understand, from the use of "go", that the speaker is not at home at the time he says it; and in

I'm going to come home now.

we understand that the addressee is taken to be in the speaker's home at the time the sentence is said, or that the place is also the addressee's home. Similarly, I can say to you

When are you going to go home?

only if I am not now in your home; and if I say

When are you going to come home?

it is understood either that I am in your house when I say it, or that it is my house too. All of these things are explainable from Hypothesis A and Hypothesis V.

But what about "bring" and "take"? In

I brought a lot of work home tonight, Hon.

"home" is the home of the subject of the verb, and similarly with

He took the documents home.

Hypothesis A seems to work, in other words, for "bring" and "take", too. Or does it? Look at sentences such as:

John took the documents home.

John took Sheila home.

The second sentence permits the interpretation that John took Sheila to *her* home. To many speakers, this last sentence could also mean that John took Sheila to *his* home, but to every speaker, that is the meaning that would come out if we were to say:

John took Sheila home with him.

Analogously,

I brought her home.

could mean that I conducted her to her home; but the sentence

I brought her home with me.

has to mean that she ended up at my place, as the sentence

I brought the documents home.

says that the documents ended up at my place.

It looks as if Hypothesis A won't do, unless the verbs "bring" and "take" are given different grammatical analyses corresponding to their different uses, and unless the relations referred to in the hypothesis are definable from the semantic representations rather than from the surface structure.

Suppose, for example, that we relate sentences like

I brought the documents home.

I took the documents home.

with their paraphrases:

I came home conveying the documents.

I went home conveying the documents.

The subject of the motion verb is the owner of the home. The same relationship is also maintained if we relate the two sentences

I brought Sheila home with me.

I took Sheila home with me.

with their paraphrases:

I came home with Sheila accompanying me.

I went home with Sheila accompanying me.

In these cases the subject of the motion verb is the same as the subject of the original sentence. In the third use of these verbs, however, they must be analyzed as causatives. The semantic representation of the two sentences

I brought Sheila home.

I took Sheila home.

will have to be something like

I enabled Sheila to come home.

I enabled Sheila to go home.

It is Sheila's home, and it is "Sheila" that is the subject of the motion verb in the paraphrase.

In short, Hypothesis A can be allowed to stand, but only with the backing of a grammatical theory which allows the coreference information needed for interpreting "home" to be determined from a semantic representation of the sentence.

But, alas, matters aren't quite that simple. It is easy to see "bring" and "take" as semantically complex, but there appears to be a similar problem with the *simple* motion verbs themselves. Consider whose homes are being talked about in the next two sentences.

Can I come home?

Can I come home with you?

For the first question, the home is *my* home, as would be predicted from Hypothesis A; and it's a question I would ask under the condition that you are at my home when I ask it, or that it's also your home, as would be predicted from Hypothesis V. But the question "Can I come home with you?" is a puzzler. The question can be appropriately asked when both speaker and addressee are away from the destination referred to in the sentence, and the "home" in question is the addressee's, not the speaker's. This means that Hypothesis A cannot stand, unless there is some paraphrase of "Can I come home with you?" that has "you" as the subject of the motion verb, and unless there is also some reason to believe that that paraphrase is close to the underlying structure of the sentence. A candidate for the paraphrase we are after is

Can I accompany you when you go home?

But our sentence has the word "come", and "come" would be inappropriate in the paraphrase. The conditions on "come" do not allow us to say things like

Are you going to come home?

when the home is the addressee's alone, and the speaker is not at the addressee's home at coding time or reference time. Exactly parallel observations could be made for sentences like these but with the participants reversed, as with

Can you come home?

Can you come home with me?

There are two problems for these sentences, one having to do with interpretations of comitative "with"-phrases in general, the other having to do with the function of "come" in comitative-phrase sentences.

It is frequently the case that the entity named by the head noun of a comitative "with"-phrase is the principal actor in the event described by the sentence, and not the companion. Thus, if there is a host/guest relationship between the Browns and the Smiths in a situation described by the sentence

The Browns had dinner with the Smiths yesterday.

the hosts are the Smiths, the guests are the Browns. In third-person motion-verb sentences like

Sheila went home yesterday.

Sheila went home with Schwartz yesterday.

it is understood that Sheila is the principal actor in the first case, the companion in the second case. I have no idea why this is so, but I know at least that it is not a phenomenon that is unique to deictic sentences. Somehow we will want to relate the sentence about Sheila's going home with Schwartz to a representation suggested by

Schwartz went home with Sheila accompanying him.

in order for the principle of Hypothesis A to make it possible to get the identity of the homeowner right.

The puzzle about the appropriateness of the verb "come" in these sentences is another matter. Notice that although the two sentences

Can you come home?

Can you go home?

have very different appropriateness conditions, the two sentences

Can you come home with me?

Can you go home with me?

have essentially the same function if they are uttered away from the speaker's home. Similar observations hold for sentences with the participants reversed. Compare the two sentences

Can I come home?

Can I go home?

with

Can I come home with you?

Can I go home with you?

An understanding of the function of "come" in these sentences will require a revision of Hypothesis V. It has to do with the use of the verb in sentences in which what is relevant is not anything about the destination of the movement, but the fact that the principal actor is one of the conversation participants, and the sentence is about something or somebody accompanying him.

Suppose that I am planning to spend a year wandering around, far from home, with no particular destination in mind, and I want to invite you to accompany me. I can say,

Would you like to go (along)?

but I could just as well say

Would you like to come (along)?

The same options are available if you are the traveller and I am asking to be invited along. I can ask either of these two questions:

Can I come (along)?

Can I go (along)?

The revised hypothesis must take into account this new condition. I should mention, incidentally, that the companion does not need to be a conversation participant, but the principal actor does. Thus, in the sense I have in mind, it's okay for me to ask if Johnny can join you on a trip by asking

Can Johnny come (with you)?

but it's not okay to ask if I can join Fred on his trip by asking

Can I come (with Fred)?

unless some of the other appropriateness conditions for "come" are satisfied.

> Hypothesis VI [Hypothesis V plus First Addendum]: "come" and "bring" also indicate motion at reference time which is *in the company of* either the speaker or the addressee.

I think that our account of the appropriateness conditions for "come" and "bring" is complete in respect to the occurrence of these verbs in simple sentences concerning which the identity and the location of the conversation participants are relevant. There is also a use of these verbs in third-person narrative, as I have already mentioned, in which the destination appropriate for "come" is a place that is somehow associated with the central character of the narrative at that point–either his location at reference time or his home base. This doesn't capture it completely, however, because it's also possible to choose a reference place–a place with which the narrator somehow associates himself and his reader's imagination–which has no particular association with a central character. Thus, if I'm talking about an uninhabited island in a little-known lake in Minnesota, I can talk about a loon "coming" there at night and about the waves "bringing" things to its shores. But I can only let this place continue to be the *deictic center* for motion verbs if I do not bring the speaker or addressee into the same discourse. After describing this island in the way I suggested, I cannot then add

> I would like to come there some day.

One of the observations that I made about the deictic center in third-person discourse is that you can only have one at a time. I pointed out that it's funny to say

> After John came to Bill's house, John and Bill together came over to Mary's house.

I suggested once that the recognition of the central character of an episode as reflected in the choice of "come" in English must have some functional similarity to the distinction maintained in the Algonkian languages and a few others between the "proximative" and "obviative" third person pronouns. Only one person (or other animate being) at a time can be referred to with the proximative pronoun, everybody else getting the obviative one.

Anyway, the final version of our account of the *deictic motion verbs* will be something like this:

> Hypothesis VII [Hypothesis VI plus Second Addendum]: "come" and "bring" also indicate, in discourse in which neither speaker nor addressee figures as a character, motion toward a place taken as the subject of the narrative, toward the location of the central character at reference time, or toward the place which is the central character's home base at reference time.

Sometimes it is said of English that the use of "come" for motion toward the addressee should be described as an instance of the speaker's taking the addressee's point of view. If assigning a deictic center can be equated with taking a point of view—as is suggested by the use in third-person discourse—then it may be that even in deictically anchored sentences, there can only be one deictic center for these verbs, within a single portion of the discourse.

The claim seems not to be true, but raising the question brings into light a number of interesting new issues. Suppose we are talking about somebody who lives half-way between our houses, and we are thinking about journeys that he might make from his house to your house and from his house to my house. (I set the situation up this way merely to rule out questions about our being close neighbors and whether his moving toward where you are is simultaneously moving toward where I am.) If both speaker and addressee can be deictic centers for "come" in the same sentence, then the addressee's-point-of-view theory about "coming to see you" won't stand. It happens to be acceptable to most speakers of English to say, in the situation I have in mind, a sentence like

> Either he'll come to your house to watch television tonight, or he'll come to my house to play ping-pong.

It also seems to be okay to say

> He'll come to your house to watch television, and then after the news he'll come to my house to play ping-pong.

But now I have to ask you what you think of these two sentences.

> He'll come to your house before he comes to my house.

> He'll come to my house after he comes to your house.

Some speakers accept both of these sentences, but a large number uniformly reject the one with "after". The hypothesis that there might be only one deictic center in conversational discourse got disconfirmed by a look at a few examples like these, but in the process I was led to this other horror. I have no idea on earth what to say about it.

It needs to be remembered that the account we ended up with is an account of the semantics of the verb "come" and "bring" in *English* (and, especially for "bring", not all dialects of English at that), and that words which are like these verbs in other languages might have some-what different appropriateness conditions prescribed for them.

In many languages, for example, the "come" and "bring" verbs are appropriate for motion toward places associated with the speaker only. In these languages, when Mother calls Junior to the dinner table, Junior says "I'm going", not "I'm coming". "Coming" is motion toward *me*, not motion toward *you*. Standard Japanese is like this, but, as I've learned from Haruo Aoki, in a great many dialects–e.g., Nagasaki–the pattern is more like what we have in English.

It also happens that the conditions for using "come" and "go" in the accompaniment sense isn't equally free in all languages. In Albanian, I've been told, one says

> Can I go (*come) with you?

> Can you come (*go) with me?

My Chinese informant tells me that, in both Cantonese and Mandarin, both options are available if the addressee is the companion and the speaker is the traveller, but if it's the other way around, the only option is

Can I go with you?

I don't know how general restrictions of this sort are, across languages, and it's difficult to find out how it works in different languages by reading their grammars. It's something I would like to be able to look into some day.

The words "come" and "go" will come up again in my discussion of social deixis, particularly in connection with what I'll be calling "taking the other fellow's point of view". By the way of preview, I point out that in some languages in which the deictic motion verbs refer basically only to the speaker, it happens that in polite or deferential language, the deictic center can be assigned to the addressee. In Mazahua, according to Don Stuart, this applies not only to the motion verbs, but also to the place-deictic words. A polite letter written in Mazahua will say something like "I wish I could come here to visit you, but I can't get away; can you go there to visit me?", where the meaning is "I wish I could go there, and I'm asking you to come here." (I've invented the example, but I believe it's not misleading.)

With my next lecture I'll return to general questions of deixis.

Postscript I: The "tag along" sense of come, provided for in the Hypothesis VI version, mentions the speaker and addressee, but in this case, the relevant conversation participants are not necessarily the speaker and addressee *at the performative level*. This is indicated by the unacceptability of the second clause in a sentence like: "Fred asked Mary to come with him to Tahiti, so she came with him."

Postscript II: David Peizer has pointed out to me some of the syntactic consequences of associating the reference place for "go" with the Source, for "come" with the Goal; I believe that Jeff Gruber has made similar observations somewhere. They have to do with the fact that, if the reference place is something which is established in the discourse, sentences in which the speaker implies ignorance of the reference place are bad. The principle predicts, therefore, that sentences like "Where did he go?" are all right, but "Where did he come?" are bad (in the motion-verb sense of "come"), and, similarly, that "He went to somewhere" and "He came from somewhere" are acceptable, while "He went from somewhere" and "He came to somewhere" are not.

DEIXIS II

My previous general lecture on deixis dealt with *place deixis* and *time deixis*. Today I will take up the topics of discourse deixis and social deixis, beginning with the former.

Discourse deixis has to do with the choice of lexical or grammatical elements which indicate or otherwise refer to some portion or aspect of the ongoing discourse–something like, for example, "the former". Most commonly, the terms of discourse deixis are taken from systems of deictic and non-deictic *time* semantics, for the very good reason that any point in a discourse can be thought of as a point in time–the time at which that portion of the discourse is encoded or decoded–with preceding portions of the discourse conceived as occurring earlier in time, later portions thought of as occurring later in time. Expressions in discourse deixis taken directly from non-deictic time semantics are words like "earlier" and "later", and phrases like "the preceding x" and "the following x". That is, an expression like "in the following paragraphs" is analogous to "in the following weeks".

A point in the development of a discourse can be taken as the *coding time*, so that such deictic time notions as the oriented tenses are completely appropriate for discourse-deictic locutions. "In the last paragraph we saw…" is an example with the discourse point taken as *general coding time*; "in the next paragraph I will show…" is an example using *encoding time*; and "in the last chapter you saw that…" is an example using *decoding time*.

The deictic time expressions "this", "next", and "last" that are appropriate for portions of discourse are those that are appropriate for calendar units in the time semantics. "In the last paragraph" is like "last week"; "in the next chapter" is like "during the next month"; and "This sentence contains five words" is a little like "This month contains three legal holidays."

There are a few discourse-deictic elements which are peculiar to written as opposed to spoken discourse. Examples are "above" and "below" in English, or their equivalents in Japanese, "izyoo" and "ika". The image in both the English case and the Japanese case is based on the written language, but two languages differ in acceptability of the written-language form in spoken discourse. In Japanese formal speechmaking, the words "izyoo" and "ika" are quite appropriate; but in English the only people allowed to refer to what they have just said as "the above" are those irritating professors who insist on reading their lectures word for word from a written text.[1]

The word "this" has the function I mentioned above, as in a sentence like "This sentence contains five words," which was said to be like the use with deictic calendric time units. A special function that it has in speech is similar to the visual gestural use in a sentence like "Hers was about this big"; what I have in mind is the use of a sentence like "She spoke about this loud," a sentence in which the degree of loudness of its performance constitutes the demonstration referred to by the demonstrative.

The demonstratives "this" and "that" have additionally their uses in referring to an immediately preceding and an immediately following portion of the discourse, respectively. The phenomenon is not limited to discourse, but to anything at all occurring close to the coding time— either something which the speaker performs or some happening which is observable at the same time by encoder and decoder. Thus, I can introduce my frog act, or I can introduce my explanation of something, by saying "This is my imitation of a frog" or "This is my explanation" respectively; similarly, I can post-announce my frog act or my explanation by saying something like "That was my imitation of a frog" or "That was my explanation." It seems to me that there is much in common with this particular usage and the distinction between the *coreferentiality* use of "this" and "that" by which, with "this" the idea is that one of the participants knows what it is that is being referred to but

---

1. Note to reader: this was not a complaint but an act of humility. I read these lectures word for word from a written text.

the other does not, and with "that" it is assumed that both encoder and decoder know what is being talked about. A passage with "this" in the function just mentioned is

> I met a friend of yours last night. Well, this guy told me some pretty interesting things about you.

A passage with "that" in the "both-of-us-know" function is

> Remember the man who sold us those football tickets? Well, that guy told me...

The forward-pointing and backward-pointing demonstratives of discourse deixis are similarly distinguished, I think, because when I say (just before giving my explanation) "This is my explanation," I know what it is but you don't; but when I say "That was my explanation," we both know what it is.

This is true in general, but the distinction is obscured by the fact that "this" also has, more so in some dialects than in others, a backward-pointing function as well as a forward-pointing function. The backward-pointing function was illustrated in the first clause of the last sentence. There appear to be tense restrictions of some sort associated with the use of "this" as opposed to "that" in backward-pointing discourse deixis, as is suggested by the fact that it is more acceptable to say "This has been an interesting course" or "That was a brilliant lecture" than to say "This was an interesting course" or "That has been a brilliant lecture."

In cases where a preceding portion of a discourse contains a list of two items, many languages have special devices for referring to the elements in the list. In English we have the words "the former" and "the latter". In a number of other languages—including French and German—the demonstratives have that function, the proximal demonstrative being used to mean "the latter", the distal demonstrative used to mean "the former".

In discourse deixis there are also sometimes special ways of referring to the encoder or the decoder, but this, I would guess, has more to do with gentility conventions about personal references in writing than with grammatical realities that should be of interest to us here. There is not much more, gentle reader, to say about discourse deixis, in the opinion of the present author, than what has already been said. (It occurs to me that it ought to be fairly easy for people to figure out how much of this lecture was delivered orally and how much was added in the writing up.)

The subject of discourse deixis can lead fairly naturally to the subject of *discourse analysis*, and that, in turn, can lead naturally to our next topic, social deixis.

A typical view of discourse analysis has it that its goal is the presentation of the total design of a text. That aspect of discourse analysis which gets suggested by the 'moving finger' or 'moving coding time' idea emphasizes the need for a technique which will allow the analyst to characterize the discourse at any point in its development. For example, it ought to be possible to choose any point in a discourse, to identify the current message, to specify what is being communicated at this point, what is being presupposed, which of its presuppositions are established in earlier portions of the discourse, which of its presuppositions are challenged or revised in later portions of the discourse, and so on.

And where discourse analysis of the sort I have in mind is applied to samples of *conversation*, the kinds of observations the analyst will find himself making will lead directly to a consideration of social deixis.

The analysis of conversation can be carried on at two levels: the one I will call *external*, the other *internal*. The external analysis of conversation deals with the mechanics of conversation—the pacing, the manner of choosing the next speaker, the pausing between and within contributions to the conversations, the devices that are used for initiating and terminating a conversation, the ways in which *clearance cues* are issued which allow the listening members of a conversational group to know that the 'floor' is clear, the ways in which a participant knows that it is his 'turn' to speak, and so on. The study of these sorts of things belongs more appropriately, I would guess, to such other disciplines as the ethnography of communication, the sociology of small-group interaction, ethnomethodology, Victor Yngve's 'state-of-mind theory' (Yngve 1970),[2] and interaction chronography (Jaffe and Feldstein 1970),[3] than to linguistics proper; but I feel sure that linguistics can profitably draw from these studies in many ways.

I believe that certain sorts of observation about the nature of conversation can probably be best understood with the help of an analogy.

Let's assume that there is a game of catch called 'conversation', a game played by throwing balls in the air one at a time. For all versions of the game, the player comes to the game with a basket full of balls, and the rule which distinguishes the game as 'conversation' rather than juggling or warfare is the rule that only one ball can be in the air at a time, no matter how many players there are. Each ball corresponds to a topic of conversation on which the player wishes to say something. The act of tossing a ball into the air corresponds to contributing something to the conversation on that topic.

Various versions of the game will turn out to be analogous to various types of real conversations. There is first of all that version of the game which corresponds to the *ideal* conversation, the type of conversation that is the model for playwrights and theorists of conversational interaction. In this version of the game, one of the players starts by picking out a ball and throwing it in the air. One of the other players watches the ball carefully, goes to the place where it is going to land, catches it, and throws it back to the first player. This goes on until the players let the ball fall to the ground, or until the original player catches it and puts it back in his basket.

That version of the game modeled the *ideal* conversation. The ball-game model of the *normal* conversation goes more like this. One player takes one of his balls and throws it into the air. The other players wait until the ball has fallen to the ground, and then one of them takes one

---

2. Victor Yngve, On Getting a Word in Edgewise, in *Papers from the Regional Meeting, Chicago Linguistic Society* 6 (1970) pp. 567–577.
3. Joseph Jaffe and Stanley Feldstein, *Rhythms of Dialogue* (New York: Academic Press, 1970).

of his balls and throws it in the air. Everybody waits for it to land, and then somebody else, maybe the first player, takes one of his balls and throws it in the air. It is important to realize that the writing of conversation rules is based on a notion of conversation that is modeled with the first game, not the second.

(Incidentally, there are other types of conversations that can be understood by analyzing their game analogs. One of these is a game I will call the *socratic dialog*. In this game there are two players, known as the *entertainer* and the *straight man*. The entertainer begins by choosing one of his balls, and throwing it high in the air. The straight man watches it carefully, waits patiently for it to land, catches it, and then hands it back to the entertainer. Another of these games is called *Meet the Press*. In this game the two players are called the *newsman* and the *administration spokesman*. The game begins by having the newsman take one of his balls and throw it directly toward the administration spokesman. The administration spokesman *pretends* to catch it, but he takes one of his own balls and throws it in the air. The newsman notices that his partner didn't catch the ball, so he retrieves it and throws it again. The administration spokesman pretends to catch it a second time, but again throws out one of his own balls. After three tries, the newsman stops retrieving the same ball and takes out another one. This one has the same fate.)[4]

The external analysis of conversation deals with such matters as: when does one participant decide to make a contribution to the conversation; how does he gain the attention of the other participants; how does a participant know when it's his turn; what does he do to guarantee that he will have a turn; how does a participant change the topic; how does the conversation get terminated; and so on.

Any of these topics offers enormous possibilities for research, and the people who work in these areas can sometimes find a lot to say about what superficially looks like an extremely small matter. Take, for

---

4. A basic flaw in my thinking was the assumption that there are conversations at all, outside of the theater, for which a player actually waits for another player's ball to land.

example, the English greeting "hello" and the hesitation-pause utterance "uh".

Harvey Sacks,[5] the ethnomethodologist at Irvine, has a great deal to say on the function in conversation of the hesitation-marker "uh". He has noticed that participants in a conversation are less tolerant of pauses if the pauses occur *between* two successive contributions to the conversation than if they occur *within* one person's contribution. The main function of "uh" is to signal "it's my turn" ("my ball is in the air"). In the middle of a contribution, the "uh" indicates that the current speaker has more to say and that the pause is not to be construed as indicating that his speech has ended. At the beginning of a contribution to the conversation, the "uh" has the function of claiming the floor. If you speak to me and I say "uh", I am indicating to you that I'm going to take my turn, but you have to wait until I think of what I want to say.

(One way of checking out the functional importance of this turn-holding syllable is to do something which violates the expectations that are associated with its normal use. I once conducted an experiment with my linguistics colleagues at Ohio State during a luncheon faculty meeting. In the middle of the meeting I said "uh," and everybody else remained silent, waiting for me to say something. I happened to be chewing food at the time, so I pointed to my cheeks and went on chewing. My conversation partners waited while I finished chewing, and looked toward me expectantly when I finally swallowed. I then took another forkful of food and resumed eating. The reaction indicated to me that having said "uh", I had claimed the floor, so the people I was in conversation with had the right to expect me eventually to have something to say. By violating that expectation, I offended some people and amused others; we all became aware of one of the techniques of conversational interaction that can be used unfairly.)

Apparently the length of the pause that is tolerated between one person's contribution to the conversation and the next person's varies from culture to culture, and, I would expect, from individual to indi-

---

5. Who, unfortunately, died shortly after this was written.

vidual. I have heard of several cases of cross-cultural difficulties between native speakers of English and speakers from other cultures in
which conversational pacing is at a more reduced tempo. The speaker
of English frequently feels the need to say over again what he has just
said, on the theory that his interlocutor's silence is due to a problem of
hearing or attention.

A particularly interesting study of one aspect of the mechanics of
conversation is Schegloff (1968),[6] based on his dissertation, *The first
five seconds*. The study is about the mechanics and functioning of the
summoning and answering elements at the beginning of a telephone
conversation–what we might refer to as the establishing of person-deictic anchoring. One of the interesting observations that Schegloff
makes about English is that certain problems of communication over
the telephone are enhanced by the fact that the word "hello" is used
both as a summons and as an answer to a summons. When there's a
bad connection, one person shouts "hello" and what he gets back is a
lot of noise and the sound of the other person shouting "hello". He
doesn't know, if he assumes the connection is bad for both partners,
whether the "hello" he has just heard is an answer to his summons, in
which case it's his turn to say what he wanted to say, or whether the person's "hello" is a summons, in which case he must say "hello" as an answer to that summons. If our language had separate words for calling
and responding, like "chemdoo" and "boogee", such a problem could
not come up.

By the *internal* analysis of conversation I mean, on the one hand, the
analysis of what conversation partners are doing to each other by
means of their contributions to the conversation and, on the other
hand, the devices by which the utterances that speakers produce establish or reflect information about the identity of the conversation partners, the nature of the social context, or the social relations between
the partners. The former has to do with conversation rules in the sense

---

6. Emanuel A. Schegloff, Sequencing in Conversational Openings, in *American
Anthropologist,* Vol. 70 (1968) pp. 1075–1095.

of Paul Grice, Bill Labov, Robin Lakoff, and George Lakoff, as well as the principles for characterizing speech acts in the style of John Searle; the latter is *social deixis*. The two are obviously closely related, since the sorts of considerations one needs to pay attention to in describing speech acts and the various types of conversational exchanges include all of what one needs to keep in mind for descriptions of social deixis.

The ways in which the quality of conversation is affected by whether or not social-deictic anchoring is established is well understood by the leaders of a social movement that has drawn a great deal of attention to itself in recent years, especially here in California, namely the *encounter group movement*. One of the techniques used by the practitioners of this movement is that of urging its participants to limit their discourse to sincere person-deictically anchored sentences in which the reference time is identical to the coding time. (They have, as you may know, less accurate ways of describing it, but there is no doubt that the use of this technique has drawn heavily from recent advances in deictic theory.) The way it works is something like this: One of the participants says something like "Life is rotten." The leader, on hearing this, says that the participant has failed to produce a sentence which satisfies the anchoring criteria. The participant tries again, this time changing it to "I am telling you now that life is rotten," The leader explains that the criteria for producing a person-deictically anchored sentence are not satisfied merely by making the performative level explicit. The participant tries again, this time saying "*My* life is rotten." The leader gets him this time on the truthfulness and reference time criteria. "Here you are," he says, "drinking organic apple juice, soaking in a hot tub, surrounded by people who love you, and you tell us that your life is rotten. How can you expect us to believe you?" Through a few more exchanges of this sort, the leader gradually gets the participant to create a sincere fully centered utterance, which is usually something like "I want you to feel sorry for me. Please come and give me a hug." At last he has produced a sentence which established a relationship between speaker and addressee that is relevant to the moment of speech.

Social deixis, then, is the study of that aspect of sentences which reflect or establish or are determined by certain realities of the social situation in which the speech act occurs. The places to look in a language for information on social deixis include: the devices for person marking, such as the pronouns of English and most other languages; the various ways of separating speech levels, as seen, for example, in the distinctions found in so many of the languages of East Asia between plain, polite, honorific and humble speech; formal distinctions in utterances of various types that depend on certain properties of the speech act participants, as shown, for example, in the imperative sentences in Biloxi, as described by Mary Haas in 1944.[7] (In this language, imperative sentences have separate forms depending on whether they are spoken by a male to an adult male, by a female to an adult male, or whether it is spoken by anybody to an adult female, or by anybody to a child.) The various ways in which names, titles, and kinship terms vary in form and usage according to the relationships among the speaker, the addressee, the audience, and the person referred to; the various ways in which linguistic performances can count as social acts, as in insults, greetings, and expressions of gratitude; the ways in which linguistic performances can accompany other social acts, such as the "There you go," of the waitress and the "Upsy daisy" of the playful father; and, lastly, the various devices that a language provides for a speaker to be able to establish and maintain a deictic anchoring with a given addressee.

This description, as you see, absorbs what I earlier called *person deixis*, as well as many aspects of the *external analysis* of conversations and many aspects of the analysis of *speech acts*.

In studying social deixis, there are various approaches that one could take. I could begin, for example, by considering grammatical forms of a particular type and exploring their functioning in conversation and the social contexts in which their use might be considered appropriate. For

---

7. Mary R. Haas, Men's and Women's Speech in Koasati (1944). Reprinted in *Language in Culture and Society: A Reader in Linguistics and Anthropology*, ed. D. H. Hymes (New York: Harper & Row, 1964).

example, we could consider the set of pronouns which a language has, or the greeting patterns that exist in the language community, and talk about the speech-act functions in which these play a role as well as the social contexts which limit or determine their appropriateness. Or instead we could take the various speech functions, such as attention-calling, thanking, identifying oneself, referring to one's addressee, etc., and, for each of these, talk about the various forms which serve this function under specific social conditions. Or, thirdly, we could take specific defined social contexts, as, for example, a conversation between two high-status individuals who have not met each other before, and discuss the linguistic forms which are appropriate in this context for carrying out the various possible speech-act functions which conversations between these two individuals could be said to exemplify. In one way or another, I will be using each of these approaches.

Suppose we begin with pronouns. In English, the words for identifying the speaker and the addressee of a conversation are simple "I" and "you", with somewhat more variety possible if the speaker is a Quaker or if the addressee is a divinity. Another complexity, to be sure, is found in the so-called first-person-plural pronoun "we", but we have already talked about that. I mentioned that it is ambiguously inclusive or exclusive of the addressee, and I discussed something about contexts in which it does not get disambiguated. There are one or two other things worth saying about this pronoun, one being that in its singular use—its use on the part of editors, clergymen and royalty—the grammatical rules of English sometimes recognize it as singular, sometimes as plural. The verb agreement processes treat it as plural, the choice of the reflexive morpheme treats it as singular: the reflexive form of singular "we" is "ourself" and not "ourselves". Another fact about English "we" that should be mentioned is that the group of individuals included in the scope of the pronoun need not all be human. In English, but not in certain other languages, it's possible for me to ask "May we come in?" when I'm speaking for me and my pet beaver.

Japanese, by comparison with English, offers a lot more variety. There are in that language a great many person-indicating words, the choice among which depends on such factors as age, sex, and social status of the conversation participants; the social relationships that hold between them; the degree of intimacy or formality of the conversation; and combinations of these factors.

To look at some examples that might be closer to home, let's take the case of the formal and informal second-person pronouns that we find in so many European languages. Following the justly famous study of Brown and Gilman[8] we can use the symbols T for the informal pronoun and V for the formal pronoun. The pronouns referring to the addressee have both symmetric and asymmetric uses in two-party conversations. The *symmetric* cases include that in which two people exchange T and that in which two people exchange V; the *asymmetric* case is the case in which one person gives the other person T but receives V from him. What the Brown and Gilman study has shown is that even in language communities which are as much in contact with each other as the French, German, and Italian, the social conditions calling for one or another of the pronoun usage patterns differ a great deal. (For details, see their article.)

According to an extremely interesting study of pronominal usage in 19th century Russian novels by Paul Friedrich,[9] there are ten factors which determine the appropriateness of one or another of the pronominal usage patterns. These are the topic of conversation, the social context, the age or sex or generation of the conversation partners, the kinship relationship between the partners, shared membership in a dialect or social group, the possession of relative jural or political authority on the part of one of the participants, and the degree of emotional solidarity between the two. What Friedrich was particularly interested in in his study was an analysis of the phenomenon he called "breakthrough", the process of changing, as a concomitant of a changing so-

8. cf. Roger Brown and Alfred Gilman, The Pronouns of Power and Solidarity, in *Style in Language*, ed. T. A. Sebeok (Cambridge, MA: MIT Press, 1960) pp. 253–276.
9. Paul Friedrich, Structural Implications of Russian Pronominal Usage, in *Sociolinguistics*, ed. W. Bright (The Hague: Mouton, 1966).

cial relationship between the two individuals involved, from one pronominal usage pattern to another.

Certain sorts of changes in these patterns do not count as breakthroughs in this sense, being determined instead by one of the other factors. The case where army officers will exchange v while talking about military matters and will later exchange t when their conversation is social is a case that is accounted for by the factor of 'topic of conversation'. An example of a breakthrough, on the other hand, is found when two officers exchanging t while having a drink together will suddenly switch to v when one of them feels insulted and issues a challenge to a duel. The sudden loss of emotional solidarity between them is reflected in the switch from exchanging t to exchanging v.

Pronominal-usage breakthroughs can occur when people are establishing a new degree of intimacy in their relationship, in which the pattern becomes one of exchanging t. When a newly-defined social equality is set up between two people, they can switch from the asymmetric pattern to the pattern of exchanging t. *Insults* can arise either by switching from v to t or by switching from t to v. A switch from v to t can indicate that the speaker withdraws respect from his addressee; a switch from t to v can indicate that the speaker rejects previous assumptions of emotional solidarity with his conversation partner.

There is sometimes a long period of fluctuation in a breakthrough. One of the types of breakthrough that occurred in Friedrich's material was what is found in the conversations of partners in a love affair.

During the period when the new relationship is not yet firmly established, there is unease and fluctuation in the use of the pronouns. This unease comes from the fear of committing one or another of the pronoun-switching insults. One partner fears that if the other expects t and receives v, he will think that the move toward greater intimacy is being resisted; on the other hand, he fears that if the other expects v and receives t, somebody is being a bit presumptuous. The pronoun usage fluctuation, and the accompanying unease, with people who are redefining their relationship is that of not knowing what the other person's expectations are.

One interesting question related to the use of pronouns in those languages which provide a two-way distinction of the sort I have been discussing is whether the users of the language do or do not have any clearly defined way of using the pronouns in conversations with God. I talked about this with some SIL missionary linguists in Mexico and found that in some of the Indian languages of Mexico it is completely obvious to the speakers that God must be addressed as T; to others it is completely obvious that God must be addressed as V. Things are not that certain for other languages. Until recently, if you addressed the Christians' God as "tu" or "vous" in French, it depended on whether you were a Protestant or a Catholic. In short, to restate the theme of the Brown and Gilman study, knowing merely that a language has a distinction between two second-person pronouns of the type called formal and informal is not at all the same as knowing that the social and emotional significance of the use of these forms might be.

The sort of breakthrough that Friedrich studied in connection with Russian pronominal usage is, of course, not limited to pronouns. There are other devices by which the participants in a conversation address or refer to each other besides the use of pronouns, such as names, titles, and kinship terms, and the appropriateness conditions for choosing among them are quite similar to those that figure in the choice of pronouns.

An example of a symmetric way of exchanging names is that by which both partners use first names, or that by which both partners use a title and the family name. An example of an asymmetric usage is the case where one calls the other by his first name but is addressed by the other with his title and last name.

Here, too, there are the same sorts of difficulties in switching from one pattern to another. Let's suppose, for example, that I have always called you Dr. Smedlap, and you have always called me Herschel. It happens that once an asymmetric naming usage has been established between two individuals, it is very difficult to change. Certain ways of bringing about the change are more difficult than others. As the one who has been at the lower end of the relationship all these years, I would find it difficult to initiate a change in either direction. It would be presumptuous of me to say "Dr. Smedlap, would you mind if I called you Sam from now on?" and it would be difficult in another way if I were to say to you "Instead of calling me Herschel, I'd prefer it if you called me Dr. Bramble from now on."

But initiating a change would be difficult for you, too. One of the things that people do in conversation, especially in the English-speaking world, is to *maintain stratification masking*. If you say to me, "Please call me Sam instead of Dr. Smedlap," the very act of saying that is an acknowledgment of the social difference that exists between us, and that is what would make it difficult for you. The change to less formality can be made easy, however, if you decide to make a joke about it. "Hey, man, let's cut this 'doctor' bit. My name is Sam." That would do it, but this time, the very act of making a joke about it might be seen as implying a greater degree of emotional solidarity than you would like. You might not want to get *that* close to Herschel Bramble.

With these last examples I've been concerned mostly with terms of address. Similar problems exist with terms of third-person reference where the choice of an appropriate term depends on the sorts of social relationships that obtain among the speaker and the addressee and the person referred to. The situation comes up as an embarassment, most typically, whenever the gentleman is expected to order dinner in a restaurant for his companion. Suppose I am in an elegant restaurant and the waiter comes up, looking at me, and asks if I am ready to order. Since in the English of people over thirty the use of a personal pronoun as a term of *first reference* is considered rude, I would find it difficult to say "*She's* going to have a cheeseburger." The clause has to have a subject, but the alternatives also seem awkward. The versions "My wife will have a cheeseburger" or "Mrs. Willoughby here will have a cheeseburger" are awkward because of the fact that it seems inappropriate and unnecessary for somebody to introduce his wife, or Mrs. Willoughby, even, to the waiter in a restaurant.

I have tried to find out what different people do in this situation, and I have come across a number of solutions. There are some men who would avoid the dilemma by speaking to the companion, expecting the waiter to overhear their conversation: "Let's see, you wanted the cheeseburger with everything, right?" Another solution is for him to order for himself whatever it is that she wants: "That'll be two cheeseburgers, please." A better solution is for him to order the same thing for both of them, and then change his mind about his own order: "That'll be two cheeseburgers. No, on second thought, make mine a carrot-and-raisin salad." The most common solution, according to a waitress I interviewed, is a strange kind of pretended formality using the phrase "the young lady". But it's also common for people to make a joke out of it: "Her ladyship will have one of your superb cheeseburgers." My point is that for people who sense the various nuances of terms of personal reference, there is no easy or natural or 'unmarked' way of choosing a third-person subject for sentences of the type you need for ordering somebody else's dinner.

Kinship terms, used for personal reference, have different versions depending on the relationship between the speaker and his addressee. The use of a possessive pronoun with a kinship term, or a kinship term plus name, depends on whether or not the two partners in the conversation belong (in reality or symbolically) in the same family. Postal has talked about this somewhere. A child refers to a certain woman as "Mommy" when he is talking to somebody who is a member of the same family, somebody like his father or his big sister, but when he is talking to somebody outside of his family, he must say "My mommy". In Japanese one tends to use the *honorific* or *honorific-endearment* kinship terms when talking to members of one's own family, but the *humble* equivalent when talking to people outside of the family.

In English, the assumptions associated with the use of a possessive pronoun with a kinship term allow the possessive to be used insincerely in some cases, cases where the relationship is perfectly clear but the speaker, probably as a joke, wishes to act as if one or another of the partners does not have the mentioned relationship to the individual referred to. I have in mind conversations between husband and wife about young daughter Peggy. When Peggy does something particularly praiseworthy, the father says to the mother, "Look at what my daughter did." When Peggy does something offensive, however, the command becomes, "Look at what your daughter did."

Attention-calling is carried out in different ways depending upon whether a person with whom one wishes to establish person-deictic anchoring is known or unknown and whether the discourse is polite or impolite. Some general titles can be used for attention-calling, others cannot. "Miss" can be used in polite attention-calling, "Mister" in impolite attention-calling, but "Mrs." not at all. The pronoun "you" can be used, but it is impolite. When the addressee is known to the speaker, a name or more specific title than "Mr." or "Miss" is appropriate. The choice between a name or a title depends on the relationship between the partners, and certain informal titles may depend on various combinations of factors. The folksy vocative "Doc" is described somewhere by Erving Goffman as combining deference and male solidarity, used only by a male to a male.

Titles can be used for address or third-person reference in English, but in many languages they can also be used for second-person reference. Sometimes there are separate forms for address and reference, as between "the Reverend" and "Reverend". Sometimes people use titles to identify themselves, but there appear to be both social class and individual variation in this. Many people use the title "Mr." when talking about themselves ("I'm Mr. Jones"), while many others could never imagine themselves doing that. The title "Dr." is always used in self-identification by medical doctors, but usually not by holders of other sorts of doctorates. If you hear somebody say "I'm Dr. Smith" you can usually assume that he's either a medical doctor or a newly minted recipient of the Ph.D. degree.

There are many ways of referring to people which can best be thought of in terms of the speaker's taking the addressee's point of view. In particular in conversation with small children, the words used for identifying members of the child's family are the words that it would be appropriate for the child to use. A mother, thus, when talking to her small child, will refer to herself as "Mommy", to her brother Will as "Uncle Willy", to her father as "Grandpa", and so on, each time taking the word which would be appropriate for the child to use rather than the word which would be appropriate for her to use. In referring to the child, the child's name is sometimes used, but if a pronoun is used, it is always "you", the pronoun that takes the speaker's point of view. A Japanese mother will refer to her small son, when talking to him, as "boku."

A different sort of thing occurs in the peculiar symmetric naming pattern between parents and children that occurs in Arabic, as I have learned from Charles Ferguson. In this case the pattern is not limited to conversation with children. A woman's children call her "Mama" but she also calls each of them "Mama." A man's children call him "Baba," but he, symmetrically, calls each of them "Baba" too.

There are several different ways in which, for the establishment of person-deictic anchoring, the speaker identifies himself to the addressee. The various patterns in English can be illustrated by "It's me," "This is Chuck Fillmore," "I'm Chuck Fillmore," "My name is Chuck Fillmore." The order I've listed them in reflects a range in how easily the addressee can identify the speaker. In the case of "It's me," my addressee must know me well enough to be able to recognize my voice. It's something that I would use only when the sound of my voice is the only evidence you have as to my identity: I'm talking on the telephone, or my hair turned gray overnight and I no longer look like my old self. At the other extreme, if I say "My name is Chuck Fillmore" I have no reason to assume that you have ever heard of me before. The one with "this" is particularly interesting. The conditions under which it is appropriate for me to introduce myself with the locution "This is Chuck Fillmore" seem to be these: (i) the communication is by voice (i.e., not by a letter, say); (ii) the communication situation is not face-to-face; and (iii) I have reason to believe that you will recognize the name. This way of introducing oneself is appropriate over the telephone, over the radio, or on television. Sometimes on television, the pretense is made that the performer/audience relationship is face-to-face, so it is just as appropriate to say "This is Walter Cronkite" as it is to say "I am Walter

Cronkite," but the former is more appropriate over the radio. The requirement that the conversation be face-to-face is not the requirement that the individuals see each other, because people meeting each other in total darkness would not use the expression with "this", nor would blind people. I would not call up some complete stranger, somebody who had no reason to know my name, and begin our conversation with "This is Chuck Fillmore." I have noticed that some telephone salespeople make use of the presupposition unfairly. About three times in the past year I've received phone calls from salespeople who begin their pitch with "Hello Charles, this is Harry Schwartz." If the conversation had not begun with an appropriate term of address, I would have suggested right away that he had the wrong number. The introduction with "this," however, added to the near appropriateness of the "Hello, Charles" had the effect of making me think that this was somebody that I was supposed to know. Out of embarassment, I would listen to him much longer than I would have if I had known instantly that it was a sales pitch.

(Remember that the "this" of the participant-identifying locutions was one of those words that switched roles between assertions and questions. "This is Harry Schwartz" means "I am Harry Schwartz," but—in American English, but apparently not in British English—"Is this Harry Schwartz?" means "Are you Harry Schwartz?" In Britain one would say "Is that Harry Schwartz?" and would regard the question "Is this Harry Schwartz?" as a part of a guessing game. It's conceivable that this use of "this" is a way of taking the addressee's point of view, because it is not appropriate in combination with a clear addressee-indicating pronoun like "you". It's okay to say "Is that you, Harry?" but not "Is this you, Harry?" when trying to get the person on the other end of the line to tell you who he is.)

The phenomenon of 'taking the other person's point of view' has come up two or three times in these lectures, and it might be interesting now to summarize the sorts of things which serve this function and to add one or two observations that have not been brought up before.

I mentioned today the special use of kinship terms when talking to children, terms which are those the child would use, not those the speaker would ordinarily use. And I also mentioned the addressee-referring use of Japanese "boku", a boy's word for "I".

I mentioned in an earlier lecture that I had learned from Don Stuart that in the Mazahua language of Mexico, a language in which the movement verbs of the "come" pattern refer basically to motion toward a location identified with the speaker, there is a special way of switching the place-deictic center from the speaker to the addressee in *deferential language*. Ordinarily one would say "*I* am *here* and people *come* to me. *You* are *there* and people *go* to you." But in deferential uses of language, as in some letters Stuart has received, one uses the place-deictic words with the poles reversed, as if "You are here, people come to you. I am over there, people go to me." William Gedney has told me that in Thai this switching of deictic centers is possible in letter-writing but not in other forms of communication. If you invite me over to your house and I accept the invitation in Thai, my answer will be something like "I will go there" if I give it over the telephone, something like "I will come here" if I get it to you by mail.

The shift of the place-deictic center in letter-writing in some languages is analogous to the way in which the authors of writings can identify the time-deictic center with the time in which the material is being read as opposed to the time at which it is being written. That is, if I am writing to you I can let the central time for the tense system of my sentences be either the time I am writing the letter or the time you are reading. Suppose, for example, that I write you a letter before you take your vacation, and I know that you will receive the letter after you return. If I say "I hope you have a good vacation," I have taken writing time as central, but if I say "I hope you had a good vacation," I have taken reading time as central. In English letter-writing conventions there are generally both possibilities, but apparently if the writer's current activities are mentioned in the letter, the writing time needs to be central. In the epistolary Latin of Cicero, by way of contrast, this was not necessary because the writer's activities at writing time were by convention assigned a past tense, the time that is past to the writing time assigned the pluperfect tense. (See R. Lakoff (1970))[10]

It has seemed to me from time to time that the gestural use of certain demonstratives is different depending on whether the speaker takes his own point of view or the addressee's. I suggested earlier that in cases of precise indication, the proximal/distal opposition for demonstratives get 'neutralized', but there might be something to say in favor of the point-of-view explanation. If I am indicating a sore tooth when talking to a dentist I can say either "It's *this* one" or "It's *that* one." I have the feeling that the second of these acknowledges the addressee's point of view.

I once even thought that a way of testing this hypothesis could be devised in connection with a non-linguistic analog of the point-of-view problem, namely the choice of ways in which we can indicate to somebody that there's a smudge on his face.

Suppose I have a smudge on my left cheek. Some people in telling me about it will point to their left cheek, others will point to their right cheek. The latter are regarding themselves as mirrors and are taking my point of view—or so I thought, anyway. (It may be that they're just having the left/right problem that some people, especially very young children, have in face-to-face interaction.) Anyway, what I thought was that if people tell me about a smudge on my left cheek by pointing to their right cheek they would be more inclined to say "It's right there" than "It's right there," and that people who tell me about it by pointing to their left cheek would be more likely to say "It's right here." Not only do I no longer have much confidence in the hypothesis, but I am unwilling to carry out the experiment. One way of doing it, one might think, is to go around, pointing to one's left cheek, and telling some people "You have a smudge right here" and telling other people "You have a smudge right there" and notice which cheek they decide to wipe off.

---

10. Robin Lakoff, Tense and its Relation to Participants, *Language*, Vol. 46 (1970) pp. 838–849.

As I mentioned earlier, other places to look for information about requirements on social contexts for linguistic performance is in the description of the various types of speech acts—such things as greeting, apologizing, insulting, promising, and giving thanks. There is no end to the examples one could give, but just to illustrate the sorts of problems that might come up, let's consider *greetings* and *thanks*.

English has a number of time-of-day greetings, and these can be specified according to whether they can be conversation-initiating (like "good morning") or conversation-terminating (like "good night") and the like. In a number of other languages, the greeting patterns reflect more sorts of social realities. A typical Zapotec pattern is one by which, when meeting somebody outdoors, one says either "Where are you going?" or "Where have you been?" Notice that in order to know how to perform a greeting in this language, you have to know where the person you are addressing lives—because only then can you know whether he's walking toward his home ("Where have you been?") or away from his home ("Where are you going?"). In the Mixe dialect studied by John and Shirley Lyons, when you meet somebody outdoors you notice whether the person is older than you or younger. If he's younger, forget it, because he'll greet you. If he's older, you notice whether he's walking uphill, downhill, or on a level. When he reaches the appropriate distance you say, as appropriate, "You are going uphill." When somebody comes to your house, you have to know where his house is, in respect to yours, in order to welcome him, because the way to welcome somebody to your home is to say "You have come downhill" or "You have come uphill" or the like.

For expressions of gratitude, let's consider just the two English expressions "Thank you" and "You're welcome." In English, but not in all languages, it is appropriate to express thanks when somebody has made a gift, performed a favor, given praise, or made an inquiry into one's health. In some languages the equivalent expression is much more limited, and in many languages one would not say "Thank you" on being praised or commended.

The response "You're welcome" is sometimes described as a kind of conditioned response to the linguistic stimulus "Thank you," but it is actually nothing of the sort. It is appropriate to say "You're welcome" when you have been thanked for a gift or a favor, but *not* when being thanked for praise or an inquiry into your health or well-being. For example, if he says to her, "You have very lovely legs" and she says "Why, thank you," he does not then say "You're welcome." If she says to him "How's your wife?" and he says "Much better, thank you," she does not then say "you're welcome."

(Incidentally, this is good to keep in mind when arguing with a behavioralist. It's common, when challenged to think of one thing which can be thought of as being a linguistic response to a purely linguistic stimulus, for the example of "You're welcome" to come up. Examples like those I just mentioned ought to convince your opponent that "You're welcome" is not an instance of a one-step conditioned response.)

SELECTED BIBLIOGRAPHY

The preceding lectures were given in the summer of 1971, and are reprinted here without revision. There has been more work done in this area of linguistics since the time these lectures were given. This select bibliography reflects the substance and range of the deictic considerations addressed in this volume. The titles listed here are by no means a complete record of these recent works on the subject. Instead, this list should simply assist those who wish to pursue the further study of deixis.

Abraham, Werner. The necessity of inserting "speaker" and "hearer" as basic categories of a practicable grammatical model. *Etudes Linguistiques* 10 (1973): 31–46.

————. Second-Language Acquisition and Deixis. The Interaction of Pragmatics and Semantics in the Universal Base Pattern of the Verbs to Come and to Go [Zweitspracherwerb und Deixis. Die Interaktion von Pragmatik und Semantik im universellen Grundmuster der Verben kommen und gehen]. *Grazer Linguistische Studien* 41 (1994): 1–17.

Abubakar, Ayuba-Tanko. The Acquisition of 'Front' and 'Back' among Hausa Children: A Study in Deixis. Diss., Teachers College Columbia University. Abstract in *Dissertation Abstracts International* 46, no. 12 (June 1986): 3702A.

Achard, Pierre. Between Deixis and Anaphora: Referring the Context to the Situation. The Operators alors and maintenant in French [Entre deixis et anaphore: le renvoi du contexte en situation. Les Operateurs "alors" et "maintenant" en francais]. In *La Deixis: Colloque en Sorbonne* 8–9 Juin 1990 [Deixis: Colloquium at the Sorbonne 8–9 June 1990], ed. Mary-Annick Morel and Laurent Danon-Boileau. Paris: Presses Universitaires de France, 1992. 583–592.

Adamson, Sylvia. From Empathetic Deixis to Empathetic Narrative: Stylisation and (De-)Subjectivisation as Processes of Language Change. *Transactions of the Philological Society* 92, no. 1 (1994): 55–88.

Afanas'eva, O. D. Communicative Inefficiency of Utterances with Situational Deixis (English Language Material) [Kommunikativnaya nedostatochnost' vyskazyvaniy, soderzhashchikh situativnyy deyksis (na materiale angliyskogo yazyka)]. *Istoriya Yazykoznanie Literaturovedenie* 44, no. 3 (July 1989): 93–96.

Agha, Asif. Grammatical and Indexical Convention in Honorific Discourse. *Journal of Linguistic Anthropology* 3, no. 2, (December 1993): 131–163.

Alfonso, Ricardo Miguel, and Jose Luis Cifuentes-Honrubia. Language and Space. Introduction to the Problems of Deixis in Spanish [Lengua y espacio. Introduccion al problema de la deixis en espanol]. *Estudios de Linguistica* 8 (1992): 217–220.

Andersson, Sven Gunnar. Proximity and Distality in the German Tense/Mood System [Proximitat und Distalitat im deutschen Tempus/Modussystem]. *Nordlyd* 22 (1994): 1–7.

Andrews, Edna. Grammar and Pragmatics: The Two Axes of Language and Deixis. In *New Vistas In Grammar: Invariance And Variation*, ed. Linda R. Waugh and Stephen Rudy. Amsterdam: John Benjamins Publishing Company, 1991. 407–413.

Angulu, Elizabeth-Mama. Componential Analysis of Hausa Verbs of Motion: Markedness and Deixis. Diss., Teachers College Columbia University. Abstract in *Dissertation Abstracts International* 46, no. 12 (June 1986): 3703A.

Ariel, Mira, and Revere D. Perkins. Deixis, Grammar, and Culture. *Journal of Pragmatics* 23 (April 1995): 455–459.

Auer, Peter. On Deixis and Displacement. *Folia Linguistica* 22, no. 3–4 (1988): 263–292.

Austin, Peter. The Deictic System of Diyari. *Pragmatics and Beyond* 3, no. 2–3 (1982): 273–284.

————. The deictic system of Diyari. In *Here and There: Cross-Linguistic Studies on Deixis and Demonstration*, ed. Jürgen Weissenborn and Wolfgang Klein. Amsterdam: John Benjamins, 1982.

Bader, Francoise. Pronominal Forms, Functions, Etymologies [Formes, fonctions, etymologies pronominales]. In *La Deixis: Colloque en Sorbonne* 8–9 Juin 1990 [Deixis: Colloquium at the Sorbonne 8–9 June 1990], ed. Mary-Annick Morel and Laurent Danon-Boileau. Paris: Presses Universitaires de France, 1992. 27–41.

Barberis, Jeanne-Marie. A Deictic Usage Proper to Oral Language: The la of Closure [Un Emploi deictique propre a l'oral: le "la" de cloture]. In *La Deixis: Colloque en Sorbonne* 8–9 Juin 1990 [Deixis: Colloquium at the Sorbonne 8–9 June 1990], ed. Mary-Annick Morel and Laurent Danon-Boileau. Paris: Presses Universitaires de France, 1992. 567–578.

Bartolucci, Giampiero, and Robert J. Albers. Deictic categories in the language of autistic children. *Journal of Autism and Childhood Schizophrenia* 4, no. 2 (March 1974): 131–141.

Bátori, István. On Verb Deixis in Hungarian. *Pragmatics and Beyond* 3, no. 2–3 (1982): 155–165.

————. On verb deixis in Hungarian. In *Here and There: Cross-Linguistic Studies on Deixis and Demonstration*, ed. Jürgen Weissenborn and Wolfgang Klein. Amsterdam: John Benjamins, 1982.

Berckmans, Paul R. In Defense of the Demonstrative/Indexical Distinction. *Logique et Analyse* 33, no. 131–132 (September–December 1990): 191–201.

Berman, Helaine A. Behind the Mask: Indexicality and Identity in Javanese Conversational Narratives. Diss., Georgetown University. Abstract in *Dissertation Abstracts International* 55, no. 11 (May 1995): 3491A–3492A.

Berthoud, Anne-Claude. Deixis, Thematization, and Determination [Deixis, thematisation et determination]. In *La Deixis: Colloque en Sorbonne* 8–9 Juin 1990 [Deixis: Colloquium at the Sorbonne 8–9 June 1990], ed. Mary-Annick Morel and Laurent Danon-Boileau. Paris: Presses Universitaires de France, 1992. 527–542.

Bluhdorn, Hardarik. Deixis and Deictics in Contemporary German [Deixis und Deiktika in der deutschen Gegenwartssprache]. *Deutsche Sprache* 21, no. 1 (1993): 44–62.

———. What Is Deixis? [Was ist Deixis?] *Linguistische Berichte* 156 (April 1995): 109–142.

Bluhdorn, Hardarik, and Anna Fuchs. Remarks on Deixis. *Linguistische Berichte* 154 (December 1994): 485–488.

Bluhdorn, Hardarik, and Kiseang Cheang. The Semantics of Deixis. An Organismic Analysis of Linguistic Deixis [Semantik der Deixis. Eine organismische Analyse sprachlicher Deixis]. *Linguistische Berichte* 150 (April 1994): 174–176.

Borillo, Andree. Some Markers of Spatial Deixis [Quelques Marqueurs de la deixis spatiale]. In *La Deixis: Colloque en Sorbonne* 8–9 Juin 1990 [Deixis: Colloquium at the Sorbonne 8–9 June 1990], ed. Mary-Annick Morel and Laurent Danon-Boileau. Paris: Presses Universitaires de France, 1992. 245–256.

Bosredon, Bernard, and Sophie Fischer. Labeling and Objects of Representation, or Impossible "ce N" [Etiquetage et objets de representation ou "ce n" impossible]. In *La Deixis: Colloque en Sorbonne* 8–9 Juin 1990 [Deixis: Colloquium at the Sorbonne 8–9 June 1990], ed. Mary-Annick Morel and Laurent Danon-Boileau. Paris: Presses Universitaires de France, 1992. 489–497.

Bourdin, Philippe. Consistency and Inconsistencies of Deicticity: The Resemanticization of Andative and Ventive Markers [Constance et inconstances de la deicticite: la resemantisation des marqueurs andatifs et ventifs]. In *La Deixis: Colloque en Sorbonne* 8–9 Juin 1990 [Deixis: Colloquium at the Sorbonne 8–9 June 1990], ed. Mary-Annick Morel and Laurent Danon-Boileau. Paris: Presses Universitaires de France, 1992. 287–307.

Bourquin, Guy. Ambiguities of Deixis [Ambiguites de la deixis]. In *La Deixis: Colloque en Sorbonne* 8–9 Juin 1990 [Deixis: Colloquium at the Sorbonne 8–9 June 1990], ed. Mary-Annick Morel and Laurent Danon-Boileau. Paris: Presses Universitaires de France, 1992. 387–399.

Brecht, Richard D. Deixis in embedded structures. *Foundations of Language* 11, no. 4 (July 1974): 489–518.

Burdach, Ana Maria, Anamary Cartes, Patricio Moreno, and Nora Rocca. Some Considerations Concerning Temporal Deictic Adverbs in English and Spanish [Algunas consideraciones en torno a los adverbios deiticos temporales en ingles y espanol]. *Revista de Linguistica Teorica y Aplicada* (RLA) 23 (1985): 163–173.

Byrne, Francis. Deixis as a Noncomplementizer Strategy for Creole Subordination Marking. *Linguistics* 26, no. 3 (1988): 335–364.

Cabrejo-Parra, Evelio. Deixis and Symbolic Operations [Deixis et operations symboliques]. In *La Deixis: Colloque en Sorbonne* 8–9 Juin 1990 [Deixis: Colloquium at the Sorbonne 8–9 June 1990], ed. Mary-Annick Morel and Laurent Danon-Boileau. Paris: Presses Universitaires de France, 1992. 409–414.

Camargo-Uribe, Angela. Who Is Who, from Where and When (Deixis in Spanish) [Del quien es quien, del donde y del cuando (La deixis en espanol)]. *Linguistica y Literatura* 9, no. 13–14 (January–December 1988): 79–92.

Campos, Jorge. Semantic Reference-Pragmatic Reference: According to Kripke [Referencia semantica-referencia pragmatica: sob Kripke]. *Letras de Hoje* 27 (September 1992): 11–24.

Carter, Anthony T. The Acquisition of Social Deixis: Children's Usages of 'Kin' Terms in Maharashtra, India. *Journal of Child Language* 11 (February 1984): 179–201.

Caubet, Dominique. Deixis, Aspect, and Modality: The Particles ha- and ra- in Moroccan Arabic [Deixis, aspect et modalite: les particules ha- et ra- en arabe marocain]. In *La Deixis: Colloque en Sorbonne* 8–9 Juin 1990 [Deixis: Colloquium at the Sorbonne 8–9 June 1990], ed. Mary-Annick Morel and Laurent Danon-Boileau. Paris: Presses Universitaires de France, 1992. 139–149.

Chang, Kyung-Hee. Semantic Analysis of Korean Deictic Terms i, gu, ce [Title in Korean; see translation]. *Ohak-Yonku* [Language Research] 16, no. 2 (December 1980): 167–184.

Chang, Suk-Jin. Deixis ui sang sung zuk ko charl (Korean) [A generative study of deixis]. *Ohak-Yonku* [Language Research] 8, no. 2 (1972): 26–43.

Chung, Yoon-Suk. *A Study of Place Deixis in English: with reference to demonstratives and deictic verbs of motion.* Seoul: Department of English: Graduate School of Seoul National University, 1988.

Chvany, Catherine V. The Oppositions [+/- deixis], [+/- distance], and [+/- discreteness] in Bulgarian and English Verbal Morphology [Oppozitsii [+/- deyksis], [+/- distantsiya] i [+/- diskretnost'] v morfologii bolgarskogo i angliyskogo glagolov]. *Supostavitelno Ezikoznanie* [Contrastive Linguistics] 15, no. 6 (1990): 5–13.

Ciapuscio, Guiomar E. Deixis and the Textual Functioning of Pronouns [La deixis y el funcionamiento textual de los pronombres]. *Revista Argentina de Linguistica* 4, no. 1–2, (March–September 1988): 25–66.

Cinque, Guglielmo. Fillmore's semantics of "come" revisited. *Lingua e Stile* 7, no. 3 (1972): 575–599.

———. On "Linguistic" Deixis [Sulla deissi "linguistica"]. *Lingua e Stile* 11, no. 1, (March 1976): 101–126.

Clark, Eve V. Normal States and Evaluative Viewpoints. *Language* 50, no. 2, (June 1974): 316–332.

————. Speaker Perspective in Language Acquisition. *Linguistics* 28, no. 6 (1990): 1201–1220.

Clark, Eve V., and C. J. Sengul. Strategies in the Acquisition of Deixis. *Journal of Child Language* 5 (October 1978): 457–475.

Cocchiarella, Nino B. Review Article: From Indices to Entities and Back Again: The Ontological Commitments of Pragmatics. *Semiotica* 103, no. 3–4 (1995): 339–347.

Collinot, Andre. Dictionary, Discourse, Deixis [Dictionnaire, Discours, Deixis]. In *La Deixis: Colloque en Sorbonne* 8–9 Juin 1990 [Deixis: Colloquium at the Sorbonne 8–9 June 1990], ed. Mary-Annick Morel and Laurent Danon-Boileau. Paris: Presses Universitaires de France, 1992. 499–506.

Cooper, Russ. That's What I'm Talking About: Discourse Level Deixis in Buhutu. *Language and Linguistics in Melanesia* 23, no. 2 (1992): 95–105.

Corazza, Eros, and Jerome Dokic. On the Cognitive Significance of Indexicals. *Philosophical Studies* 66, no. 2 (May 1992): 183–196.

Corblin, Francis. Demonstratives and Naming [Demonstratif et nomination]. In *La Deixis: Colloque en Sorbonne* 8–9 Juin 1990 [Deixis: Colloquium at the Sorbonne 8–9 June 1990], ed. Mary-Annick Morel and Laurent Danon-Boileau. Paris: Presses Universitaires de France, 1992. 439–456.

Cortes, Colette. Deixis and Text Types in German [Deixis und Textsorten im Deutschen]. *Etudes Germaniques* 49, no. 2, (April–June 1994): 205–206.

Cortes, Colette, and Helge Szabo. Anaphora or Deixis? Deixis or Determination? A Study of the Oppositions among the German Morphemes es, dies, das [Anaphore ou deixis? Deixis ou determination? Etudes des oppositions entre les morphemes allemands: "es", "dies", "das"]. In *La Deixis: Colloque en Sorbonne* 8–9 Juin 1990 [Deixis: Colloquium at the Sorbonne 8–9 June 1990], ed. Mary-Annick Morel and Laurent Danon-Boileau. Paris: Presses Universitaires de France, 1992. 551–565.

Cotte, Pierre. From Deixis to Argumentation: The Case of Adverbial "the" in Contemporary English [De la deixis a l'argumentation: le cas du "the" adverbial de l'anglais contemporain]. In *La Deixis: Colloque en Sorbonne* 8–9 Juin 1990 [Deixis: Colloquium at the Sorbonne 8–9 June 1990], ed. Mary-Annick Morel and Laurent Danon-Boileau. Paris: Presses Universitaires de France, 1992. 593–602.

Coulmas, Florian. Some remarks on Japanese deictics. In *Here and There: Cross-Linguistic Studies on Deixis and Demonstration*, ed. Jürgen Weissenborn and Wolfgang Klein. Amsterdam: John Benjamins, 1982

Crepin, Andre. Determinatives in Old English: Anaphoric se and Deictic thes [Determinatifs en vieil-anglais: l'anaphorique "se" et le deictique "thes"]. In *La Deixis: Colloque en Sorbonne* 8–9 Juin 1990 [Deixis: Colloquium at the Sorbonne 8–9 June 1990], ed. Mary-Annick Morel and Laurent Danon-Boileau. Paris: Presses Universitaires de France, 1992. 53–63.

Danell, Karl Johan. Notes on the Competition between ceci and cela in Modern French [Notes sur la concurrence entre ceci et cela en francais moderne]. *Studia Neophilologica* 62, no. 2 (1990): 195–212.

Danon-Boileau, Laurent. What "That" Means: The Lessons of Clinical Observation [Ce que "ça" veut dire: les enseignements de l'observation clinique]. In *La Deixis: Colloque en Sorbonne* 8–9 Juin 1990 [Deixis: Colloquium at the Sorbonne 8–9 June 1990], ed. Mary-Annick Morel and Laurent Danon-Boileau. Paris: Presses Universitaires de France, 1992. 415–425.

Danziger, Eve. Out of Sight, Out of Mind: Person, Perception, and Function in Mopan Maya Spatial Deixis. *Linguistics* 32, no. 4–5 (1994): 885–907.

Danziger, Eve, and Revere D. Perkins. Deixis, Grammar, and Culture. *Linguistics* 31, no. 5 (1993): 977–980.

Dasgupta, Probal. Pronominality and Deixis in Bangla. *Linguistic Analysis* 22, no. 1–2 (1992): 61–77.

Davidse, Kristin, and Anna Fuchs. Remarks on Deixis. *Functions of Language* 2, no. 1 (1995): 125–126.

Davis, Philip W., and Ross Saunders. Bella Coola Nominal Deixis. *Language* 51, no. 4 (December 1975): 845–858.

———. Bella Coola Deictic Roots. *International Journal of American Linguistics* 42, no. 4 (October 1976): 319–330.

De Carvalho, Paulo. Deixis and Grammar [Deixis et grammaire]. In *La Deixis: Colloque en Sorbonne* 8–9 Juin 1990 [Deixis: Colloquium at the Sorbonne 8–9 June 1990], ed. Mary-Annick Morel and Laurent Danon-Boileau. Paris: Presses Universitaires de France, 1992. 95–103.

De Moor, E. The Vocative as a Deictic Element. A Neglected Aspect of Theatrical Discourse [Le Vocativ comme element deictique. Un Aspect neglige du discours theatral]. *Orientalia Lovaniensia Periodica* 21 (1990): 213–240.

Delmas, Claude. Deixis and Structuring: A Contrastive Study between English and Spanish [Deixis et structuration: etude contrastive entre l'anglais et l'espagnol] In *La Deixis: Colloque en Sorbonne* 8–9 Juin 1990 [Deixis: Colloquium at the Sorbonne 8–9 June 1990], ed. Mary-Annick Morel and Laurent Danon-Boileau. Paris: Presses Universitaires de France, 1992. 123–133.

Den Boer, Monica. Deictic References to Space and Time in Criminal Evidence. *International Journal for the Semiotics of Law* [Revue Internationale de Semiotique Juridique] 7, no. 21 (1994): 295–310.

Devonish, Hubert, and Jean Charles Pochard. On the Diversification in the Function of Deictic Markers: A Study of a, da and dem in the Jamaican Creole Noun Phrase. *English World-Wide* 9, no. 2 (1988): 213–226.

Dezhe, Laslo. Typological Questions of Deixis [Tipologicheskie voprosy deyksisa]. *Facultas Philosophica* 225 (1979): 77–82.

Dingwall, Silvia. "Hello. This Is Sally's Answering Machine." Deixis in Answerphone Messages. *Bulletin Suisse de Linguistique Appliquee* 62, (October 1995): 129–153.

Djamouri, Redouane. The Use of the Deictics zi and zhi in the Shang Inscriptions [Emploi des deictiques zi et zhi dans les inscriptions Shang]. *Cahiers de Linguistique Asie Orientale* 23 (1994): 107–118.

Door, Jorgen, and Jorgen Christian Bang. Deixis, Gender, & Core Contradictions. *Working Papers on Language, Gender and Sexism* 1, no. 2, Sept (1991): 53–71.

Dry, Helen Aristar. Timeline, Event Line, and Deixis. *Language and Style* 21, no. 4 (fall 1988): 399–410.

Dubos, Ulrika. Deixis, Temporality, and the Concept of "Situation" [Deixis, temporalite et le concept de "situation"]. In *La Deixis: Colloque en Sorbonne* 8–9 Juin 1990 [Deixis: Colloquium at the Sorbonne 8–9 June 1990], ed. Mary-Annick Morel and Laurent Danon-Boileau. Paris: Presses Universitaires de France, 1992. 319–330.

Edmonson, Barbara. Peirce's Theory of Signs and Its Relation to Deixis in Language. *Human Mosaic* 11, no. 2 (fall 1977): 1–14.

Ehlich, Konrad. Scientific Texts and Deictic Structures. In *Cooperating With Written Texts: The Pragmatics And Comprehension Of Written Texts*, ed. Dieter Stein. Berlin: Mouton de Gruyter, 1992. 201–229.

Ehrich, Veronika. Da and the System of Spatial Deixis in German. *Pragmatics and Beyond* 3, no. 2–3 (1982): 43–63.

———. Da and the system of spatial deixis in German. In *Here and There: Cross-Linguistic Studies on Deixis and Demonstration*, ed. Jürgen Weissenborn and Wolfgang Klein. Amsterdam: John Benjamins, 1982.

Eloy, Jean-Michel. Questions on Deixis regarding the Picard Definite Article [Questions sur la deixis a propos de l'article defini picard]. In *La Deixis: Colloque en Sorbonne* 8–9 Juin 1990 [Deixis: Colloquium at the Sorbonne 8–9 June 1990], ed. Mary-Annick Morel and Laurent Danon-Boileau. Paris: Presses Universitaires de France, 1992. 75–82.

Euler, Wolfram. A Near Deictic Demonstrative in the Northern Indo-European Languages—Its Late Dialectal Foundations [Ein nahdeiktisches Demonstrativum in den nordlichen indogermanischen Sprachen—seine voreinzelsprachlichen Grundlagen]. *Linguistica Baltica* 2 (1993): 15–29.

Evans, Nicholas. 'Wanjh! Bonj! Nja!': Sequential Organization and Social Deixis in Mayali Interjections. *Journal of Pragmatics* 18 (September 1992): 225–244.

Faerch, Claus. A Contrastive Description of Deixis in Danish and English. *Papers and Studies in Contrastive Linguistics* 7 (1977): 61–72.

Fernandez-Vest, M.M. Jocelyne. Deixis, Anaphora, Dialogic Thematization [Deixis, anaphore, thematisation dialogique]. In *La Deixis: Colloque en Sorbonne* 8–9 Juin 1990 [Deixis: Colloquium at the Sorbonne 8–9 June 1990], ed. Mary-Annick Morel and Laurent Danon-Boileau. Paris: Presses Universitaires de France, 1992. 543–550.

Feuillet, Jack. The Structuring of Spatial Deixis [La Structuration de la deixis spatiale]. In *La Deixis: Colloque en Sorbonne* 8–9 Juin 1990 [Deixis: Colloquium at the Sorbonne 8–9 June 1990], ed. Mary-Annick Morel and Laurent Danon-Boileau. Paris: Presses Universitaires de France, 1992. 233–243.

Fillmore, Charles J. Toward a theory of deixis. *University of Hawaii Working Papers in Linguistics* 3 (April 1971): 219–242.

Fludernik, Monika. Shifters and Deixis: Some Reflections on Jakobson, Jespersen, and Reference. *Semiotica* 86, no. 3–4 (1991): 193–230.

Forbes, Isabel. This, That, and Yon in Modern Scots ["This", "That" et "Yon" en ecossais moderne]. In *La Deixis: Colloque en Sorbonne* 8–9 Juin 1990 [Deixis: Colloquium at the Sorbonne 8–9 June 1990], ed. Mary-Annick Morel and Laurent Danon-Boileau. Paris: Presses Universitaires de France, 1992. 83–88.

Fourie, D. J. Mbalanhu Absolute and Demonstrative "Pronouns". *Languages of the World* 2, no. 7 (1993): 14–22.

Fox, Barbara A. Contextualization, Indexicality, and the Distributed Nature of Grammar. *Language Sciences* 16 (January 1994): 1–37.

Francois, Frederic. The Child and Deixis [L'Enfant et la deixis.] In *La Deixis: Colloque en Sorbonne* 8–9 Juin 1990 [Deixis: Colloquium at the Sorbonne 8–9 June 1990], ed. Mary-Annick Morel and Laurent Danon-Boileau. Paris: Presses Universitaires de France, 1992. 427–437.

Fries, Udo. Text Deixis in Early Modern English. In *Studies In Early Modern English*, ed. Dieter Kastovsky. Berlin: Mouton de Gruyter, 1994. 111–128.

Fuchs, Anna. Verbal Aspects and Deixis [Aspectos verbal e deixis]. *Cadernos de Estudos Linguisticos* 15, July–Dec (1988): 87–109.

Fuchs, Milena-Zic. On Contrasting Expressions of Spatial Deixis in Croatian and English. *Studia Romanica et Anglica Zagrabiensia* 36–37 (1991–1992): 93–102.

Furrow, Melissa. Listening Reader and Impotent Speaker: The Role of Deixis in Literature. *Language and Style* 21, no. 4 (fall 1988): 365–378.

Gachelin, Jean-Marc. Gender and Deixis in Southwestern Dialects. *Neuphilologische Mitteilungen* 92, no. 1 (1991): 83–93.

Gahl, Susanne, Andy Dolbey, and Christopher Johnson, eds. *Proceedings of the 20th Annual Meeting of the Berkeley Linguistics Society: Dedicated to the Contributions of Charles J. Fillmore.* Berkeley: Berkeley Linguistics Society, 1994.

Galton, Herbert. Deixis in Syntactic Development [Deixis in syntaktischer Entwicklung]. *Folia Linguistica* 11, no. 3–4 (1977): 217–230.

Gandour, Jackson Thomas. On the Deictic Use of Verbs of Motion Come and Go in Thai. *Anthropological Linguistics* 20, no. 9 (December 1978): 381–394.

Gildea, Spike. The Development of Tense Markers from Demonstrative Pronouns in Panare (Cariban). *Studies in Language* 17, no. 1 (1993): 53–73.

Ginina, Stefaniya. Deixis and Noun Definiteness in Bulgarian and Serbo-Croatian [Deiksis i opredelenost na imenata v bulgarskiya i surbokhurvatskiya ezik]. *Supostavitelno Ezikoznanie* [Contrastive Linguistics] 5, no. 6 (1980): 32–37.

Giordano, Paola. Personal Deixis in Dramatic Communication: An Analysis of Plautus's Miles Gloriosus [La deissi personale nella comunicazione drammatica: analisi del Miles Gloriosus di Plauto]. *Lingua e Stile* 24, no. 3 (September 1989): 409–433.

Greenberg, Joseph H. The Second Person Is Rightly So Called. In *Principles And Prediction: The Analysis Of Natural Language: Papers In Honor Of Gerald Sanders*, ed. Mushira Eid and Gregory Iverson. Amsterdam: John Benjamins Publishing Company, 1993. 9–23.

Grenoble, Lenore. Spatial Configurations, Deixis and Apartment Descriptions in Russian. *Pragmatics* 5, no. 3 (September 1995): 365–385.

Grewendorf, Gunther. Deixis and Anaphora in German Tense [Deixis und Anaphorik im deutschen Tempus]. *Papiere zur Linguistik* 1 (1982): 47–83.

Groussier, Marie-Line. Deixis and Metaphoric Representation of Time in Old English: The Case of "Todaeg"/"Today" [Deixis et representation metaphorique du temps en vieil-anglais: le cas de "todaeg"/"today"]. In *La Deixis: Colloque en Sorbonne* 8–9 Juin 1990 [Deixis: Colloquium at the Sorbonne 8–9 June 1990], ed. Mary-Annick Morel and Laurent Danon-Boileau. Paris: Presses Universitaires de France, 1992. 331–344.

Hagege, Claude. The System of the Anthropophor and Its Morphogenetic Aspects [Le Systeme de l'anthropophore et ses aspects morphogenetiques]. In *La Deixis: Colloque en Sorbonne 8–9 Juin 1990* [Deixis: Colloquium at the Sorbonne 8–9 June 1990], ed. Mary-Annick Morel and Laurent Danon-Boileau. Paris: Presses Universitaires de France, 1992. 115–122.

Hanks, William F. The Evidential Core of Deixis in Yucatec Maya. *Papers from the Regional Meetings, Chicago Linguistic Society* 20 (1984): 154–172.

———. The Indexical Ground of Deictic Reference. *Papers from the Regional Meetings, Chicago Linguistic Society* 25, no. 2 (1989): 104–122.

———. *Referential Practice: language and lived space among the Maya.* Chicago: University of Chicago Press, 1990.

———. The Indexical Ground of Deictic Reference. In *Rethinking Context: Language as an Interactive Phenomenon*, ed. Alessandro Duranti and Charles Goodwin. Cambridge, England: Cambridge University Press, 1992. 43–76.

———. Metalanguage and Pragmatics of Deixis. In *Reflexive Language: Reported Speech And Metapragmatics*, ed. John A. Lucy. Cambridge, England: Cambridge University Press, 1993. 127–157.

Harman, Ian P. Teaching Indirect Speech: Deixis Points the Way. *English Language Teaching Journal* 44, no. 3 (July 1990): 230–238.

Harris, Richard J., and William F. Brewer. Deixis in memory for verb tense. *Journal of Verbal Learning and Verbal Behavior* 12, no. 5 (1973): 590–597.

Hartmann, Dietrich. Deixis and Anaphora in German Dialects: The Semantics and Pragmatics of Two Definite Articles in Dialectal Varieties. *Pragmatics and Beyond* 3, no. 2–3 (1982): 187–207.

———. Deixis and anaphora in German dialects: The semantics and pragmatics of two definite articles in dialectical varieties. In *Here and There: Cross-Linguistic Studies on Deixis and Demonstration*, ed. Jürgen Weissenborn and Wolfgang Klein. Amsterdam: John Benjamins, 1982.

Harweg, Roland. Deictic and Adeictic Tenses [Deiktische und adeiktische Zeitstufen]. *Zeitschrift fur romanische Philologie* 90, no. 5–6 (1974): 499–525.

———. Deixis and Sensory Data [Deixis und Sinnesdaten]. *Acta Linguistica Academiae Scientiarum Hungaricae* 25, no. 3–4 (1975): 379–401.

———. The Forms of Zeigen and Their Relation to Deixis: A Study in Pragmatics [Formen des Zeigens und ihr Verhaltnis zur Deixis: Ein Beitrag zur Pragmatik]. *Zeitschrift fur Dialektologie und Linguistik* 43, no. 3 (1976): 317–337.

Hauenschild, Christa. Demonstrative Pronouns in Russian and Czech—Deixis and Anaphora. *Pragmatics and Beyond* 3, no. 2–3 (1982): 167–186.

———. Demonstrative pronouns in Russian and Czech—Deixis and Anaphora. In *Here and There: Cross-Linguistic Studies on Deixis and Demonstration*, ed. Jürgen-Weissenborn and Wolfgang Klein. Amsterdam: John Benjamins, 1982.

Haukioja, Timo. Pointing in Sign Language and Gesture: An Alternative Interpretation. *Language and Communication* 13, no. 1 (January 1993): 19–25.

Haverkate, Henk. Deictic Categories as Mitigating Devices. *Pragmatics* 2, no. 4 (December 1992): 505–522.

Hazelkorn, Leena-Tuulikki. The Role of Deixis in the Development of Finno-Ugric Grammatical Morphemes. *Ohio State University Working Papers in Linguistics* 27 (May 1983): 89–139.

Heeschen, Volker. Some Systems of Spatial Deixis in Papuan Languages. *Pragmatics and Beyond* 3, no. 2–3 (1982): 81–109.

———. Some systems of spatial deixis in Papuan Languages. In *Here and There: Cross-Linguistic Studies on Deixis and Demonstration*, ed. Jürgen Weissenborn and Wolfgang Klein. Amsterdam: John Benjamins, 1982.

Herman, David. Textual You and Double Deixis in Edna O'Brien's *A Pagan Place*. *Style* 28, no. 3 (fall 1994): 378–410.

Hill, Clifford. Up/down, front/back, left/right. A contrastive study of Hausa and English. In *Here and There: Cross-Linguistic Studies on Deixis and Demonstration*, ed. Jürgen Weissenborn and Wolfgang Klein. Amsterdam: John Benjamins, 1982.

Hosokawa, Hirofumi. Japanese Demonstratives ko-, so-, and a-. *Georgetown Journal of Languages and Linguistics* 1, no. 2 (spring 1990): 169–178.

Hottenroth, Priska-Monika. The System of Local Deixis in Spanish. *Pragmatics and Beyond* 3, no. 2–3 (1982): 133–153.

———. The system of local deixis in Spanish. In *Here and There: Cross-Linguistic Studies on Deixis and Demonstration*, ed. Jürgen Weissenborn and Wolfgang Klein. Amsterdam: John Benjamins, 1982.

Houweling, Frans. Deictic and Anaphoric Tense Morphemes. *Journal of Italian Linguistics* 7, no. 1 (1982): 1–30.

Hullen, Werner. Reflections on Person-Deixis, Time-Deixis, and Place-Deixis in a Text [Uberlegungen zur Personen-Deixis, Zeit-Deixis und Orts-Deixis im Text]. *Anglistik und Englischunterricht* 27 (1985): 53–62.

Huls, Carla, Wim Claassen, and Edwin Bos. Automatic Referent Resolution of Deictic and Anaphoric Expressions. *Computational Linguistics* 21, no. 1 (March 1995): 59–79.

Ionescu-Ruxandoiu, Liliana. Suggestions for a Pragmatic Interpretation of Deixis in Spoken Daco-Romanian, Part 1 [Sugestii pentru interpretarea pragmatica a unor deictice in dacoromana vorbita (I)]. *Studii si cercetari lingvistice* 43, no. 6 (November–December 1992): 523–532.

Ivanova, A. N. The Words togda, teper', and potom in the Sentence and Text [Slova "togda"-"teper'"-"potom" v predlozhenii i tekste]. *Russkii yazyk v shkole* 80, no. 2 (March–April 1993): 86–90.

Jaggar, Philip J., and Malami Buba. The Space and Time Adverbials NAN/CAN in Hausa: Cracking the Deictic Code. *Language Sciences* 16 (October 1994): 387–421.

Janssen, Theo A. J. M. Tenses and Demonstratives: Conspecific Categories. In *Conceptualizations And Mental Processing In Language*, ed. Richard A. Geiger and Brygida Rudzka Ostyn. Berlin: Mouton de Gruyter, 1993. 741–783.

Jarvella, Robert J., and Wolfgang Klein, eds. *Speech, Place, and Action: Studies in Deixis and Related Topics*. John Wiley and Sons, 1982.

Johnston, Margaret A. Developing Concepts of Person and the Acquisition of Person Deixis. Diss., University of Manchester, England. Abstract in *Dissertation Abstracts International* 51, no. 1 (July 1990): 454B.

Jonasson, Kerstin. Is the Reference of Proper Nouns a Matter of Deixis? [La Reference des noms propres releve-t-elle de la deixis?] In *La Deixis: Colloque en Sorbonne* 8–9 Juin 1990 [Deixis: Colloquium at the Sorbonne 8–9 June 1990], ed. Mary-Annick Morel and Laurent Danon-Boileau. Paris: Presses Universitaires de France, 1992. 457–470.

Jordan, Rita R. An Experimental Comparison of the Understanding and Use of Speaker-Addressee Personal Pronouns in Autistic Children. *British Journal of Disorders of Communication* 24 (August 1989): 169–179.

Jouve, Dominique. "Now" and Temporal Deixis ["Maintenant" et la deixis temporelle]. In *La Deixis: Colloque en Sorbonne* 8–9 Juin 1990 [Deixis: Colloquium at the Sorbonne 8–9 June 1990], ed. Mary-Annick Morel and Laurent Danon-Boileau. Paris: Presses Universitaires de France, 1992. 355–363.

Kapitan, Tomis. I and You, He* and She*. *Analysis* 52 (April 1992): 125–128.

Karl, Sornig, and Veronika Ehrich. Here and Now: Studies on Local and Temporal Deixis in German [Hier und Jetzt. Studien zur lokalen und temporalen Deixis im Deutschen]. *Grazer Linguistische Studien* 39–40 (1993): 257–261.

Kleiber, Georges. Anaphora-Deixis: Two Rival Approaches [Anaphore-deixis: deux approches concurrentes]. In *La Deixis: Colloque en Sorbonne* 8–9 Juin 1990 [Deixis: Colloquium at the Sorbonne 8–9 June 1990], ed. Mary-Annick Morel and Laurent Danon-Boileau. Paris: Presses Universitaires de France, 1992. 613–626.

Klein, Wolfgang. 'Where is here?' Preliminaries to a Study of Local Deixis [Wo ist hier? Praliminarien zu einer Untersuchung der lokalen Deixis] *Linguistische Berichte* 58 (December 1978): 18–40.

Kryk, Barbara. The Pragmatics of Deixis in English and Polish. *Papers and Studies in Contrastive Linguistics* 20 (1985): 35–44.

Kurzon, Dennis. Signposts for the Reader: A Corpus-Based Study of Text Deixis. *Text* 5, no. 3 (1985): 187–200.

Lakoff, Robin. Remarks on 'this' and 'that'. *Papers from the Regional Meetings, Chicago Linguistic Society* 10 (1974): 345–356.

Larochette, Joe. Temporal Deixis in French [La Deixis temporelle en francais]. *Cahiers de l'Institut de Linguistique de Louvain* 5, no. 4 (1981): 65–72.

Larsen, Thomas W. Deictic and Non-Deictic Directionals in Awakatek. *Funcion* 15–16, (December 1994): 169–210.

Launey, Michel. When Only Demonstratives Designate: Predicates and Deictics in "Classical" Nahuatl [Quand seuls les demonstratifs designent: predicats et deictiques en nahuatl "classique"]. In *La Deixis: Colloque en Sorbonne* 8–9 Juin 1990 [Deixis: Colloquium at the Sorbonne 8–9 June 1990], ed. Mary-Annick Morel and Laurent Danon-Boileau. Paris: Presses Universitaires de France, 1992. 221–232.

Lazard, Gilbert, and Louise Peltzer. Deixis in Tahitian [La Deixis en tahitien]. In *La Deixis: Colloque en Sorbonne* 8–9 Juin 1990 [Deixis: Colloquium at the Sorbonne 8–9 June 1990], ed. Mary-Annick Morel and Laurent Danon-Boileau. Paris: Presses Universitaires de France, 1992. 209–219.

LeBlanc, Julie. The Linguistics of Enunciation and the Concept of Deictics [La Linguistique de l'enonciation et le concept de deictique]. *Linguistica* 31 (1991): 31–40.

Lemarechal, Alain. Deixis and the Accession of Parts of Speech to Substantivity and Actantial Functions [Deixis et accession des parties du discours a la substantivite et aux fonctions actancielles]. In *La Deixis: Colloque en Sorbonne* 8–9 Juin 1990 [Deixis: Colloquium at the Sorbonne 8–9 June 1990], ed. Mary-Annick Morel and Laurent Danon-Boileau. Paris: Presses Universitaires de France, 1992. 105–113.

Leonard, Anne-Marie. Deixis [La Deixis]. *Journal of French Language Studies* 3, no. 2 (September 1993): 244–246.

Letoublon, Francoise. Spatio-Temporal Deixis and the Verb System: The Case of Ancient Greek [La Deixis spatio-temporelle et le systeme verbal: le cas du grec ancien]. In *La Deixis: Colloque en Sorbonne* 8–9 Juin 1990 [Deixis: Colloquium at the Sorbonne 8–9 June 1990], ed. Mary-Annick Morel and Laurent Danon-Boileau. Paris: Presses Universitaires de France, 1992. 265–276.

Lo-Cascio, Vincenzo. Temporal Deixis and Anaphora in Sentence and Text: Finding a Reference Time. *Journal of Italian Linguistics* 7, no. 1 (1982): 31–70.

Lyons, John. *Semantics,* 2 volumes. Cambridge: Cambridge University Press, 1977.

———. Deixis and Modality. *Sophia Linguistica* 12 (1983): 77–117.

Madray-Lesigne, Francoise. The Here and the Elsewhere of the Person in Discourse. Some Affinities among Persons, Tenses, and Moods in French [L'Ici et l'ailleurs de la personne en discours. Quelques affinites entre personnes, temps et modes en francais]. In *La Deixis: Colloque en Sorbonne* 8–9 Juin 1990 [Deixis: Colloquium at the Sorbonne 8–9 June 1990], ed. Mary-Annick Morel and Laurent Danon-Boileau. Paris: Presses Universitaires de France, 1992. 401–408.

Maillard, Michel. How a Deictic Attains to the Generic: From French *ca* to Seychellois *sa*: The Law of the Three States [Comment un deictique accede au generique. Du "ca" francais au "sa" Seychellois: la loi des trois etats]. In *La Deixis: Colloque en Sorbonne* 8–9 Juin 1990 [Deixis: Colloquium at the Sorbonne 8–9 June 1990], ed. Mary-Annick Morel and Laurent Danon-Boileau. Paris: Presses Universitaires de France, 1992. 65–74.

Maisel, Linda J. Variation in Q'eqchi' (Q'eqchi' Mayan): Four Compound Deictic Forms and Their Role in Structuring Discourse. Diss., University of Pennsylvania, Philadelphia. Abstract in *Dissertation Abstracts International* 54, no. 6 (December 1993): 2136–A.

Malotki, Eckehart. Hopi Person Deixis. *Pragmatics and Beyond* 3, no. 2–3 (1982): 223–252.

———. Hopi Person deixis. In *Here and There: Cross-Linguistic Studies on Deixis and Demonstration*, ed. Jürgen Weissenborn and Wolfgang Klein. Amsterdam: John Benjamins, 1982.

Malsch, Derry L., and Kathleen M. Lant. On "Normal State" Deixis. *Linguistic Inquiry* 8, no. 4 (fall 1977): 744–746.

Marchello-Nizia, Christiane. The Evolution of the System of Demonstratives in French [L'Evolution du systeme des demonstratifs en francais]. In *La Deixis: Colloque en Sorbonne* 8–9 Juin 1990 [Deixis: Colloquium at the Sorbonne 8–9 June 1990], ed. Mary-Annick Morel and Laurent Danon-Boileau. Paris: Presses Universitaires de France, 1992. 43–52.

Mark, David M., and Michael D. Gould. Wayfinding Directions as Discourse: A Comparison of Verbal Directions in English and Spanish. *Multilingua* 11, no. 3 (1992): 267–291.

Markey, T. L. Deixis and the u-Perfect. *Journal of Indo-European Studies* 7, no. 1–2 (spring-summer 1979): 65–75.

Marriott, Stephanie Markman. Deixis in Context: A Study of the Distribution of the English Demonstratives This, That, Here and There in Naturally-Occurring Discourse. Diss., University of Essex, England. Abstract in *Dissertation Abstracts International* 53, no. 5 (November 1992): 1501A–1502A.

Martin, Eusebia H., and Andres A. Perez-Diez. Pronominal Deixis in the Chimane of Eastern Bolivia [Deixis Pronominal en el Chimane del Oriente Boliviano]. *International Journal of American Linguistics* 56, no. 4 (October 1990): 574–579.

Mazzoleni, Marco. Deictic Locatives, Deixis am Phantasma, Systems of Orientation [Locativi deittici, Deixis am Phantasma, sistemi di orientamento]. *Lingua e Stile* 20, no. 2 (June 1985): 217–246.

McCarthy, Michael. It, This and That. In *Advances in Written Text Analysis*, ed. Malcolm Coulthard. London, England: Routledge, 1994. 266–275.

McCawley, James D. Speech Acts and Goffman's Participant Roles. *Proceedings of the Eastern States Conference on Linguistics* (ESCOL) 1, (1984): 260–274.

McNeill, David, Justine Cassell, and Elena T. Levy. Abstract Deixis. *Semiotica* 95, no. 1–2 (1993): 5–19.

Meunier, Andre. Subject of Deixis and Modal Support [Sujet de la deixis et support modal]. In *La Deixis: Colloque en Sorbonne* 8–9 Juin 1990 [Deixis: Colloquium at the Sorbonne 8–9 June 1990], ed. Mary-Annick Morel and Laurent Danon-Boileau. Paris: Presses Universitaires de France, 1992. 375–386.

Mittwoch, Anita. Sentences, Utterance Boundaries, Personal Deixis and the E-Hypothesis. *Theoretical Linguistics* 12, no. 2–3 (July–November 1985): 137–152.

Moeschler, Jacques. Temporal Reference and Deixis: Toward a Milnerian Approach [Reference temporelle et deixis: vers une approche milnerienne]. *Travaux neuchatelois de linguistique* (TRANEL) 17 (July 1991): 97–122.

Monnerie, Annie. Deixis [La Deixis]. *Francais dans le Monde* 33, no. 258 (July 1993): 82–83.

Morel, Mary-Annick. Presentatives in French [Les Presentatifs en francais]. In *La Deixis: Colloque en Sorbonne* 8–9 Juin 1990 [Deixis: Colloquium at the Sorbonne 8–9 June 1990], ed. Mary-Annick Morel and Laurent Danon-Boileau. Paris: Presses Universitaires de France, 1992. 507–517.

Moreno, Patricio F. Spatial Deixis in French and Spanish [Deixis espacial en frances y espanol]. *Revista de linguistica teorica y aplicada* (RLA) 23 (1985): 157–162.

Mosel, Ulrike. Local Deixis in Tolai. *Pragmatics and Beyond* 3, no. 2–3 (1982): 111–132.

———. Local Deixis in Tolai. In *Here and There: Cross-Linguistic Studies on Deixis and Demonstration*, ed. Jürgen Weissenborn and Wolfgang Klein. Amsterdam: John Benjamins, 1982.

Muhlhausler, Peter, and Anna Fuchs. Remarks on Deixis. *Journal of Literary Semantics* 24, no. 3 (October 1995): 231–232.

Naumann, Bernd, and Gabriele Maria Diewald. Deixis and Text Types in German [Deixis und Textsorten im Deutschen]. *Leuvense Bijdragen* 82, no. 4 (December 1993): 532–536.

Net, Mariana. The Literary Text-Speech Act, Deictization, Metalanguage [Le texte litteraire-enonciation, deictisation, metalangage]. *Revue Roumaine de Linguistique* 33, no. 3 (May–June 1988): 147–150.

Nguyen, Phu-Phong. Deixis in Vietnamese [La Deixis en vietnamien]. In *La Deixis: Colloque en Sorbonne* 8–9 Juin 1990 [Deixis: Colloquium at the Sorbonne 8–9 June 1990], ed. Mary-Annick Morel and Laurent Danon-Boileau. Paris: Presses Universitaires de France, 1992. 177–186.

Nikolaeva, T. M. Deictic Particles and the Isolated Situation [Deykticheskie chastitsy i izolirovannaya situatsiya]. *Russian Linguistics* 9, no. 2–3 (1985): 281–288.

Njejimana, Gregoire. Discourse Deixis in Kirundi Folktales. Diss., Teachers College Columbia University. Abstract in *Dissertation Abstracts International* 50, no. 12 (June 1990): 3935A.

Nunberg, Geoffrey. Two Kinds of Indexicality. *Ohio State University Working Papers in Linguistics* 40 (July 1992): 283–301.

———. Indexicality and Deixis. *Linguistics and Philosophy* 16, no. 1 (February 1993): 1–43.

Opalka, Hubertus. Representations of Local Ni-Deixis in Swahili in Relation to Buhler's "Origo des Zeigfelds". *Pragmatics and Beyond* 3, no. 2–3 (1982): 65–79.

———. Representations of local Ni-deixis in Swahili in Relation to Bühler's "Origo des Zeigfelds". In *Here and There: Cross-Linguistic Studies on Deixis and Demonstration*, ed. Jürgen Weissenborn and Wolfgang Klein. Amsterdam: John Benjamins, 1982.

Orsolini, Margherita. Episodic Structure in Children's Fantasy Narratives: "Breakthrough" to Decontextualised Discourse. *Language and Cognitive Processes* 5, no. 1 (1990): 53–79.

Ostertag, Gary John. Reference and Indexicality. Diss., City University of New York. Abstract in *Dissertation Abstracts International* 55, no. 7 (January 1995): 1993–A.

Paris, Marie-Claude. Demonstratives and Person in Standard Chinese [Demonstratifs et personne en chinois standard]. In *La Deixis: Colloque en Sorbonne* 8–9 Juin 1990 [Deixis: Colloquium at the Sorbonne 8–9 June 1990], ed. Mary-Annick Morel and Laurent Danon-Boileau. Paris: Presses Universitaires de France, 1992. 167–175.

Parret, Herman. The Speech Act as Deictization and Modalization [L'Enonciation en tant que deictisation et modalisation]. *Langages* 18, no. 70 (June 1983): 83–97.

———. Deixis and Shifters after Jakobson. In *New Vistas in Grammar: Invariance and Variation*, ed. Linda R. Waugh and Stephen Rudy. Amsterdam: John Benjamins Publishing Company, 1991. 321–340.

Pasierbsky, Fritz. On the Historical Development of Person Deixis in Chinese [Zur historischen Entwicklung der Personendeixis im Chinesichen]. *Pragmatics and Beyond* 3, no. 2–3 (1982): 253–272.

———. Zur historischen Entwicklung der Personendeixis im Chinesischen. In *Here and There: Cross-Linguistic Studies on Deixis and Demonstration*, ed. Jürgen Weissenborn and Wolfgang Klein. Amsterdam: John Benjamins, 1982.

Perkins, Revere D. *Deixis, Grammar, and Culture.* Amsterdam: John Benjamins Publishing Company. 245pp.

Perret, Michele. The Now and Here of Textual Reference [Or et ci de reference textuelle]. In *La Deixis: Colloque en Sorbonne* 8–9 Juin 1990 [Deixis: Colloquium at the Sorbonne 8–9 June 1990], ed. Mary-Annick Morel and Laurent Danon-Boileau. Paris: Presses Universitaires de France, 1992. 579–582.

Perrot, Jean. Monstration, Definiteness, and Anaphora/Cataphora in Hungarian

[Monstration, definitude et anaphore/cataphore en hongrois]. In *La Deixis: Colloque en Sorbonne* 8–9 Juin 1990 [Deixis: Colloquium at the Sorbonne 8–9 June 1990], ed. Mary-Annick Morel and Laurent Danon-Boileau. Paris: Presses Universitaires de France, 1992. 135–138.

Petiot, Genevieve. Naming and Discourse Strategies [Denomination et strategies discursives]. In *La Deixis: Colloque en Sorbonne* 8–9 Juin 1990 [Deixis: Colloquium at the Sorbonne 8–9 June 1990], ed. Mary-Annick Morel and Laurent Danon-Boileau. Paris: Presses Universitaires de France, 1992. 479–487.

Pick, Herbert L., Jr., and Linda P. Acredolo, eds. *Spatial Orientation: Theory, Research, and Application.* New York and London: Plenum Press, 1983

Pochard, J. C., and H. Devonish. Deixis in Caribbean English-Lexicon Creole: A Description of A, Da and De. *Lingua* 69, no. 1–2, (June 1986): 105–120.

Portine, Henri. Remarks on the Analysis of Verbal Tenses by J. Damourette and E. Pichon and on E. Minkowski's Study of the Phenomenology of Time: On the I-Here-Now [Remarques sur l'analyse des temps verbaux par J. Damourette et E. Pichon et sur l'etude de la phenomenologie du temps de E. Minkowski: sur le moi-ici-maintenant]. In *La Deixis: Colloque en Sorbonne* 8–9 Juin 1990 [Deixis: Colloquium at the Sorbonne 8–9 June 1990], ed. Mary-Annick Morel and Laurent Danon-Boileau. Paris: Presses Universitaires de France, 1992. 309–317.

Pryor, John. Deixis and Participant Tracking in Botin. *Language and Linguistics in Melanesia* 21, no. 1–2 (1990): 1–29.

Renzi, Lorenzo. Personal Deixis and Its Social Use [La deissi personale e il suo uso sociale]. *Studi di Grammatica Italiana* 15 (1993): 347–390.

Rhodes, Richard A. 'We Are Going to Go There': Positive Politeness in Ojibwa. *Multilingua* 8, no. 2–3 (1989): 249–258.

Ricca, Davide. 'Go' and 'Come' in the Romance and Germanic Languages: From Aktionsart to Deixis [Andare e venire nella lingue romanze e germaniche: dall'Aktionsart alla deissi]. *Archivio Glottologico Italiano* 76, no. 2 (1991): 159–192.

———. The Deictic Verb Pair andare/venire in Italian: Conditions of Use and Variabilities [Le Couple de verbes deictiques "andare"/"venire" en italien: conditions d'emploi et variabilites]. In *La Deixis: Colloque en Sorbonne* 8–9 Juin 1990 [Deixis: Colloquium at the Sorbonne 8–9 June 1990], ed. Mary-Annick Morel and Laurent Danon-Boileau. Paris: Presses Universitaires de France, 1992. 277–286.

Rivarola, Jose-Luis. Who Is "We"? [¿Quien es nosotros?] *Estudios de Linguistica* 2 (1984): 201–206.

Roberts, Lawrence D. Perry on Indexical Semantics and Belief States. *Communication and Cognition* 26, no. 1 (1993): 77–96.

Rousseau, Andre. Deixis: A Problem of Logic and Philosophy of Language [La Deixis: un probleme de logique et de philosophie du langage]. In *La Deixis: Colloque en Sorbonne* 8–9 Juin 1990 [Deixis: Colloquium at the Sorbonne 8–9 June 1990], ed. Mary-Annick Morel and Laurent Danon-Boileau. Paris: Presses Universitaires de France, 1992. 365–374.

Rugaleva, Anelya. The Structure of Deictic Signs: Possessive Pronouns in Russian. *Russian Language Journal* [Russkii-Yazyk] 34, no. 117 (winter 1980): 25–42.

Sauvageot, Serge. Concerning the Expression of Deixis in Some Languages of the West Atlantic Group (Black Africa) [De l'expression de la deixis dans quelques langues du groupe ouest-atlantique (afrique noire)]. In *La Deixis: Colloque en Sorbonne* 8–9 Juin 1990 [Deixis: Colloquium at the Sorbonne 8–9 June 1990], ed. Mary-Annick Morel and Laurent Danon-Boileau. Paris: Presses Universitaires de France, 1992. 151–155.

Savchuk, G. V. The Evaluative Component of the Meaning of Spatial Phraseologisms [Otsenochnyy komponent znacheniya prostranstvennykh frazeologicheskikh edinits]. *Russkii yazyk v shkole* 82, no. 4 (July–August 1995): 71–73.

Schiffer, Stephen. Descriptions, Indexicals, and Belief Reports: Some Dilemmas (But Not the Ones You Expect). *Mind* 104 (January 1995): 107–131.

Schiffrin, Deborah. Between Text and Context: Deixis, Anaphora, and the Meaning of then. *Text* 10, no. 3 (1990): 245–270.

Sennholz, Klaus. The Fundamentals of Deixis [Grundzuge der Deixis]. *BBS, Bochumer Beitrage zur Semiotik* 9 (1985): 1–303.

Sherzer, Joel. Verbal and Nonverbal Deixis: The Pointed Lip Gesture among the San Blas Cuna. *Language in Society* 2, no. 1 (April 1973): 117–131.

Shields, Kenneth, Jr. The Role of Deictic Particles in the IE Personal Pronoun System. *Word* 45, no. 3, (December 1994): 307–315.

Shopen, Timothy, ed. *Language Typology and Syntactic Description: Vol. III: Grammatical categories and the lexicon.* Cambridge: Cambridge University Press, 1985

Silverstein, Michael. Relative Motivation in Denotational and Indexical Sound Symbolism of Wasco-Wishram Chinookan. In *Sound Symbolism*, ed. Leanne Hinton, Johanna Nichols, and John Ohala. Cambridge, England: Cambridge University Press, 1994. 40–60.

Sims-Williams, Nicholas. The Triple System of Deixis in Sogdian. *Transactions of the Philological Society* 92, no. 1 (1994): 41–53.

Sitta, Georg, and Dagmar Schmauks. Review Article: Deixis in the Human-Machine Interaction: Multimedia Referent Identification through Natural and Simulated Pointing Gestures [Deixis in der Mensch-Maschine-Interaktion: Multimediale Referentenidentifikation durch naturliche und simulierte Zeigegesten] (see abstract of review in this issue). *Semiotica* 96, no. 3–4 (1993): 319–334.

———. Review Article: Deixis and Pointing Gestures. *Semiotica* 96, no. 3–4 (1993): 319–334.

Smith, John Charles. A Pragmatic View of French Deixis. *York Papers in Linguistics* 14 (December 1989): 263–278.

———. Features, Markers, and Underspecification: Application to Deixis [Traits, marques et sous-specification: application a la deixis]. In *La Deixis: Colloque en Sorbonne* 8–9 Juin 1990 [Deixis: Colloquium at the Sorbonne 8–9 June 1990], ed. Mary-Annick Morel and Laurent Danon-Boileau. Paris: Presses Universitaires de France, 1992. 257–264.

Sprenger-Charolles, Liliane. Concerning Certain Deictic Uses of the Definite Determiner [A propos de certains usages deictiques du determinant defini]. In *La Deixis: Colloque en Sorbonne* 8–9 Juin 1990 [Deixis: Colloquium at the Sorbonne 8–9 June 1990], ed. Mary-Annick Morel and Laurent Danon-Boileau. Paris: Presses Universitaires de France, 1992. 519–526.

Tamba, Irene. Demonstratives and Personals in Japanese: Deixis and Double Structuring of the Discourse Space [Demonstratifs et personnels en japonais: Deixis et double structuration de l'espace discursif]. In *La Deixis: Colloque en Sorbonne* 8–9 Juin 1990 [Deixis: Colloquium at the Sorbonne 8–9 June 1990], ed. Mary-Annick Morel and Laurent Danon-Boileau. Paris: Presses Universitaires de France, 1992. 187–195.

Taylor, Paul Michael. Tobelorese Deixis. *Anthropological Linguistics* 26, (spring 1984): 102–122.

Ter-Meulen, Alice G. B. Demonstrations, Indications and Experiments. *Monist* 77 (April 1994): 239–256.

Tfouni, Leda Verdiani, and Roberta L. Klatzky. A Discourse Analysis of Deixis: Pragmatic, Cognitive, and Semantic Factors in the Comprehension of 'This', 'That', 'Here' and 'There'. *Journal of Child Language* 10 (February 1983): 123–133.

Thomieres, Daniel, Laurent Danon-Boileau, and Mary-Annick Morel. Deixis [La Deixis]. *Langues Modernes* 86, no. 3 (1992): 63–64.

Tokunaga, Misato. Affective Deixis in Japanese: A Case Study of Directional Verbs. Diss., University of Michigan, Ann Arbor. Abstract in *Dissertation Abstracts International* 47, no. 6 (December 1986) 2148A.

Tournadre, Nicolas. Deixis in Tibetan: Some Remarkable Facts [La Deixis en tibetain: quelques faits remarquables]. In *La Deixis: Colloque en Sorbonne* 8–9 Juin 1990 [Deixis: Colloquium at the Sorbonne 8–9 June 1990], ed. Mary-Annick Morel and Laurent Danon-Boileau. Paris: Presses Universitaires de France, 1992. 197–207.

Truner, Ken, and Anna Fuchs. Remarks on Deixis. *IRAL* 32, no. 1 (February 1994): 87–88.

Tucker, Paul. Displaced Deixis and Intersubjectivity in Narrative: Linear and Planar Modes. *Journal of Literary Semantics* 22 (April 1993): 45–67.

Van Schooneveld, Cornelis H. Praguean Structure and Autopoiesis: Deixis as Individuation. In *New Vistas in Grammar: Invariance and Variation*, ed. Linda R. Waugh and Stephen Rudy. Amsterdam: John Benjamins Publishing Company, 1991. 341–362.

Vanelli, Laura. The Deictic Mechanism and the Deixis of Discourse [Il meccanismo deittico e la deissi del discorso]. *Studi di Grammatica Italiana* 10 (1981): 293–311.

Varley, Rosemary. Deictic Terms, Lexical Retrieval, and Utterance Length in Aphasia: An Investigation of Inter-Relations. *European Journal of Disorders of Communication* 28, no. 1 (1993): 23–41.

Veden'kova, M. S. On the Problem of Studying Signs of Personal Deixis [Do pitannya vivchennya znakiv osobovogo deiksisu]. *Movoznavstvo* 12 (July–August 1978): 32–36.

Vlad, Carmen. Deixis and Referential Ambiguity in the Poetic Text [Deixis si ambiguitate referentiala in textul poetic]. *Studii si cercetari lingvistice* 41 (May–June 1990): 187–191.

Webber, Bonnie Lynn. Structure and Ostension in the Interpretation of Discourse. *Language and Cognitive Processes* 6, no. 2 (May 1991): 107–135.

Wiederspiel, Brigitte. The Proper Noun: A Third Type of Reference? [Le Nom propre: un 3e type de reference?] In *La Deixis: Colloque en Sorbonne* 8–9 Juin 1990 [Deixis: Colloquium at the Sorbonne 8–9 June 1990], ed. Mary-Annick Morel and Laurent Danon-Boileau. Paris: Presses Universitaires de France, 1992. 471–478.

Wilkins, David P. Interjections as Deictics. *Journal of Pragmatics* 18 (September 1992): 119–158.

Wilkins, David P., and Deborah Hill. When "go" Means "come": Questioning the Basicness of Basic Motion Verbs. *Cognitive Linguistics* 6, no. 2–3 (1995): 209–259.

Wunderli, Peter. Personal Deixis in Romance Languages: The Problem of Internal Structure [La Deixis personnelle dans les langues romanes: le probleme de la structuration interne]. *Vox Romanica* 49–50 (1990–1991): 31–56.

Wunderlich, Dieter. Pragmatics, speaking situation, deixis [Pragmatik, Sprechsituation, Deixis]. *LiLi, Zeitschrift fur Literaturwissenschaft und Linguistik* 1 no. 1/2 (1971): 153–190.

Zechner, Klaus, and Dagmar Schmauks. Deixis in Man-Machine Interactions. Multimedia Referents; Identification through Natural and Simulated Pointed Gestures [Deixis in der Mensch-Maschine-Interaktion. Multimediale Referentenidentifikation durch naturliche und simulierte Zeigegesten]. *Grazer Linguistische Studien* 37 (spring 1992): 152–155.

Ziegler, Jurgen. The Source and the Foundation Problem of Deixis [Die origo und das Grundlagenproblem der Deixis]. *Deutsche Sprache* 17, no. 3 (1989): 193–205.

Zribi-Hertz, Anne. From Deixis to Anaphora: Some Milestones [De la deixis a l'anaphore: quelques jalons]. In *La Deixis: Colloque en Sorbonne* 8–9 Juin 1990 [Deixis: Colloquium at the Sorbonne 8–9 June 1990], ed. Mary-Annick Morel and Laurent Danon-Boileau. Paris: Presses Universitaires de France, 1992. 603–612.

Zupnik, Yael-Janette. A Pragmatic Analysis of the Use of Person Deixis in Political Discourse. *Journal of Pragmatics* 21 (April 1994): 339–383.